NEIT] WEAK NOR OBTUSE

JAKE GOLDSMITH

Sagging
Meniscus

Set in Trump Mediaeval with LaTeX.

ISBN: 978-1-952386-39-8 (paperback)
ISBN: 978-1-952386-40-4 (ebook)
Library of Congress Control Number: 2022934951

Sagging Meniscus Press
Montclair, New Jersey
saggingmeniscus.com

For Mum, Dad, and Ellen

'We are all so afraid, we are all so alone, we all so need from the outside the assurance of our own worthiness to exist.'

—Ford Maddox Ford, *The Good Soldier* (1915).

'We live in a world of abstractions, of bureaus and machines, of absolute ideas and of crude messianism. We suffocate among people who think they are absolutely right, whether in their machines or in their ideas.

'And for all who can live only in an atmosphere of human dialogue and sociability, this silence is the end of the world.'

—Albert Camus, 'The Century of Fear' (*Combat*, November 21, 1946).

Contents

Preface to the Second Edition   *i*

Foreword: Treading Water, by William Fear   *iii*

Author's Introduction   *vi*

The Struggle for Home   *1*

In Abundance: Redux   *18*

The Failures of Discourse   *29*

People of Responsibility   *52*

Why I Write, What I Would Write   *66*

Correspondence, Love   *81*

The End of Chronicity   *101*

NEITHER WEAK NOR OBTUSE

PREFACE TO THE SECOND EDITION

I originally self-published this memoir via Amazon. Finding a publisher takes some effort and I pursued what limited connections I could find, but eventually was fine in settling to just have the book exist. I wanted to have a book that would encapsulate more or less everything I had to say about how my life, illness, and disability have shaped my thought. This is me and what I think. I intended it to act as an epitaph. The stereotype of elders writing their memoirs suits me; it just comes to me a lot sooner. I have a delicate life, where I am motivated to summarise who I am.

A testimony for whatever reason. It doesn't, finally, need justifying.

I wrote the book as a forecast. My thoughts generally on illness and eventually having to contend with an early death have not been much altered by any finality coming closer, or health becoming worse, but rather things come to a sharp relief or intensity.

After first publishing my memoir, I created The Barbellion Prize: an international book prize for disabled authors. Thanks to the internet people can be easy to contact, and so I was able to develop a few connections to then make this grassroots entity that I currently administer mostly from my bedroom into a success, and find support. A prize such as The Barbellion Prize had not really existed before—which was unsurprising to me if still alarming. I am unable to work or do much thanks to illness, so the prize becomes my main focus or distraction. And then thanks to the prize I was lucky enough to be noticed by literary sorts who took an interest in what I had to say.

I've now been given the opportunity to revisit my memoir, polish it, rewrite small sections and give a clearer demonstration of what I want to convey. Not much fundamentally has changed since I first published it besides necessary edits to grammar and the usual editorial clarifications.

I wish to acknowledge Guillermo Stitch for being a salutary editor, as well as my dearest friends Murphy Davis, Max Dirlik-Brown, William Fear, Akshat Khare, Blaine McCartney, Nikola D. Mironija, Eric Osterberg, Wendy Shanel Behrend, and Kooper Wilson.

I also wish to thank David Collard, Elizabeth Ferretti, Mette Ivers, and Riva Lehrer for their conversation and solidarity.

The title of the book paraphrases a line from Boris Pasternak, in a letter he sent to Albert Camus. It should make sense by the end.

—Jake Goldsmith, March 2022

FOREWORD: TREADING WATER

There is much that is said and written in the name of philosophy which operates at a remove from life. I refer to that variety of thought which seeks to divorce itself from the practical questions of life, and how to live. Jake Goldsmith's most recent work, which you are about to read, is exempt from this charge, as it deals with matters of life and living. It speaks of a quiet persistence and passing, of the acceptance and rejection of infirmity. His work is permeated by an opalescent refusal to give up, and instead commits to a search for truth and meaning, in a world which seems to provide none.

Some call this the art of living—it seems to me as good a term as any. It is this that I so admire about Jake's writing. It is haunted by a difficult question which demands an answer. Once I was driving Jake back to his home and asked him a question I realised I'd never thought to ask him: 'Do you think your interest in philosophy has anything to do with your illness?' He replied 'Of course, because without it I drown.' He didn't need to explain what this meant: I knew him well enough by then to understand.

Since birth, Jake has been ill: constantly medicated and plagued by routine clinical suffering, but most importantly, he has always been faced with the near-certainty of an abbreviated lifespan. Jake has cystic fibrosis, often abbreviated to CF. CF is a chronic, life-limiting condition which results from specific genetic faults in two genes which code for the CFTR[1] protein. The CFTR protein is involved in maintaining and controlling mucus membranes in many of the body's systems, particularly the lungs and digestive system. In a normal person, CFTR controls these membranes, but in a CF patient, the membranes become thicker than normal, and the patient will usually have severe respiratory difficulties, as well as increased vulnerability to lung infections. The life expectancy for a CF patient is around forty-two in countries with strong healthcare infrastructures, but many die long before this. There is no cure, and the new generation of drug treatments like Lumacaftor and Ivacaftor are supposedly ineffective against Jake's CF, because of the rarity of his mutation.[2] In Jake's case, his illness has decreased his lung function to between twenty and thirty percent, which makes many things I take for granted in my own life impossible.

Most people adopt an attitude towards their impending death that is essentially evasion or disbelief. For the purposes of someone who has not had the misfortune of having to live with a chronic illness like Jake's, death is merely a concept you observe in the world which crucially, only ever seems to happen to other people. To some, the inherent truth and necessity for death is a thought that either does not penetrate, or is not allowed to. It's much easier, after all, to merely live with the delusion that it won't happen to you—somehow. I firmly believe that this delusion is one that most people maintain as a way of coping, though they may deny its existence if asked. Jake's experience of living is constantly in resistance to death—to tread the water that threatens, with its infinite depths, an eternal drowning.

[1] CFTR—Cystic Fibrosis Transmembrane Conductance Regulator
[2] To the knowledge of his doctors, Jake's CFTR mutations are totally unique in combination, and have never been documented together at once before in another patient.

Jake has never been afforded this luxury of ignorance, and as a result, he's had to grow up somewhat more quickly than most. Long before I set about the business of serious reading, Jake would spend most of his free time at school in the library. From the many authors he would go on to read, one emerged early on, to which Jake would apprentice himself, in a way: Albert Camus. There is much I would like to say about Camus, and how his work influenced Jake, but the most important and foundational thing that Jake found in Camus was his mission. That is, a commitment to finding truth in the face of absurdity, without collapsing before the feet of nihilism. In the meantime, Jake has set about accomplishing a similar mission: to continue to live and to think—to push the rock up the hill, if only to watch it roll back down.

Therefore, what *Neither Weak Nor Obtuse* offers us is not merely critical, but essential: the unique perspective on a life lived in defiance of death.

—William Fear

AUTHOR'S INTRODUCTION

I am very ill. That would be the first and most obvious thing to know.

I have something of a haughty and self-important motivation for writing a memoir, being relatively young, as I have the persistent weight of illness stunting my time to speak. I need a model of myself—to have a promotion of my worth—and so here is no small attempt at a testament to my life and constitution. This work is a show of my growth, of what I love, and some diagnosis as to why I would love those particular things.

This model doesn't have a remedial end, even if one could be discerned, but at least has something—by medical necessity—of an intellectual and physical prognosis.

There's reason for cautious clarification. I'm having to revisit things and grasp my life as I can, without pedantry, and neither can I exist comfortably in forgetful and easy living—as attractive as that might be.

I revisit things to show some awareness of my past faults, for a lack of care or empathy which pervaded, somewhat, the troubles of my youth as it would with many.

I once witnessed a man who claimed to have read all of Jonathan Swift's satire, but was still an arrogant and brutish so-and-so who would belittle anyone who did not do well in secondary school or further education. Arrogance comes easily if one can set themselves apart from their peers just by knowledge accumulation, and I could at least see that somewhere in a younger me. Hubris and immaturity seem more apparent then, even if the lens that sees is blurred by time. I want to have in mind as the rest is written a correction of attitude or tone if not of all I contain. To be read as humble and with a necessary deprecation is my pressing wish.

There are things that can be ordered, reasoned, or finely accounted, but there are those things which are incompatible. As Kierkegaard reminds us, a thinker without paradoxes is a lover without feelings. I will try to show what I feel, with all those addled contradictions, for what is perhaps a final time.

I could follow the path of abandonment found in Rimbaud,[3] which attracts me on the harder days, or I could find my steadfastness in different ways when it comes to what I will be describing. To befit my well-being in this shortened life of mine, I am better disposed to engage in personal readings of philosophy and literature than to be caught in the meticulousness of study. I was disgusted, worn-out, made weary and drained by university life and formal education. I failed to see why I was putting so much time and energy into the studious road when I was such an unpleasant student: talking beyond what I needed to, not staying in-line with a syllabus and at least half-appearing an arrogant young man who thought himself above his station.

Only the factual constraints of my health, my lack of wealth, parental wishes,[4] and not being able to be some free-

---

[3] Arthur Rimbaud (1854–1891), French poet, a known libertine and restless soul who travelled extensively after ending his literary career at the age of 21.

[4] Before I went to university my parents had high hopes for the prospect of me being less educationally regimented and more able to expand my learning horizons, as I seemed to be limited within secondary education. Unfortunately university was not for me, considering my

wheeling layabout kept me from packing up my things and leaving more expediently. But eventually the relevant people knew of my dilemma and helped me to escape.

I can only express gratitude and love for all their understanding and affection.

I may never reach the stage when I know what I want to do with my future—if it exists. But I do want to write, and that is all—for myself and anyone who'll read. I have no need for a long and aggravating study of canonical figures to then improve my perception or outlook on literature and life.

To live like that, with deadlines and a need to be tidy, did very little to suit my bodily circumstances. Being freed of the need to conform to a system I struggle to appreciate leads to a more pleasant experience, and a lot less trouble. I had plans to move to Bergen in Norway to study. But with my time as it is, it would surely be better to just visit the place casually. The problems with either of these callings (a life of action or not) are different, and I feel I can more easily, and with a healthier heart, better manage idleness and my own bounded freedom than always being busy: physical business being something I have never appreciated. For a person whose only real aim is to write—if not, to do nothing—college or university would become unhelpful beyond (what the Americans would refer to as) the sophomore year. By that time one would know that further wisdom, not the compilation of information, comes from a personal and indulgent reading of, say, Goethe, or Montaigne, and not the dry dissection, or vivisection, of impersonal work in a lab-setting—and from getting out in the world and living. Most

---

health as well as the narrow nature of my university course, and while my parents were at first enthusiastic for me to continue my studies, I was unable to. Eventually we all understood and I left university.

of the rest of scholarship in academic philosophy, history, even literature, amounts to something paltry. Not so much dead, but *lifeless* authors in unread journals. It has the misfortune (a great one considering how worthy the subject can be) of being for prim, pallid and uninspiring young men who will end up either teaching or devoting maybe 30 years of their sterile lives to investigating some miserably obscure facet of life, unless they take the initiative to do something more inspired and less set in drudgery. That said, I will not besmirch the better name of teachers or professors. There are those of a different variety and process to whom I owe the deepest of gratitude. But to be taught in the scholastic setting is something I'm averse to. The educational life is otherwise used as a stepping-stone by the proto-student to secure some sort of work. Sure, scholarship is necessary; but it is not for me. So I write, without care for scholarly enterprise, and I try to relax for the remaining years in my rarer setting of neither needing nor being able to do things. In the final analysis, I felt I had to leave formal study. My health had suffered and I could not have continued. But I can at least say I did enjoy some of the company.

Of what my writing would be, then: fundamentally it is a difficult demonstration of my personal journey, faced with many interior and exterior problems. It cannot overcome or outpace these challenges, but explores how I might contend with them given what is possible. The first few sections deal with my views on philosophy, thinking, and discourse. They are a little divorced from *the phenomenology of illness*, though nonetheless linked, while the latter sections deal more directly with living with illness. It is a portrait of my life, so if you want to skip the more academic considerations you may go to the penultimate section.

I was given a touching description by a distant American friend: 'Dostoyevsky's Underground Man tempered by the measured humanity of Camus' Dr Bernard Rieux'.[5] I hope I can maintain this measure until my last words, as it would be an appreciable legacy.

[5] Dr. Bernard Rieux is the narrator and main character of Albert Camus' *La Peste (The Plague)*. A practical man, Rieux struggles ceaselessly against the plague in the city of Oran despite his fatigue, his unbelief, and signs that his efforts are having little effect.

THE STRUGGLE FOR HOME

It will take a little while before I express clearly what a deadly, chronic illness means for my inner feeling and how I relate that to those who are closest to me. I will first address what illness means for my thinking in more abstract terms—as it ties in so inextricably with my political and philosophical discourse. These first few sections concern my identity and things that at a glance could seem unrelated to medicine and illness. But all of my discourse results directly from my being so ill. I will start with how I relate to my immediate environment . . .

I never had real emotion for my home; what I would call really moving emotion. I did so for the contents of my house, my family, especially pets, books, and the immediate surroundings where I lived; so you could say I cared for my home in that sense. But not for a nation or even so much a culture. After a while this scornful contrarianism, whether it was my fault or not, whether it was justified or not, was no longer comforting or productive. I certainly didn't appreciate the prevalent sense of class consciousness present in Britain, at all levels, its imperial history, or its economy, but the fact that there were lots of things to dislike shouldn't have meant I disliked everything. What I have always appreciated, at least in where I am from, were idiosyncrasies, small details, something just slightly amusing, with a general but meagre thankfulness that I was at

least not someplace utterly dire. The problem, in this awareness, came in elevating my own character with the help of
outside assurances, which was something I found I needed.
But ultimately I was only ever interested in land, nation, or
British culture and its practices in an offhand way. I was especially fearful of those who loved culture too much. They
showed their hand historically, and it wasn't the best of results. What I was passionate about was personal. It was not
purely theoretical or abstract. It was what others held in
their hands, oral histories, the sensual, but given life and
experience. When I came up against these things, I was
left a little empty. I wanted the tangibility that others described when they spoke of all these objects and practices
they loved, but that I felt estranged from.

It was as if descriptions of character were *hyped*, and I
had unmet expectations I knew were not overblown. I dis-
owned most optimism, so had I really fallen to raising my
hopes too high?

How am I to sustain myself in any sort of contentedness
if I cannot do it alone, where so many theories or ideas about
interior conduct fall short, yet I find most of my outside options unhelpful? Passion for stretches of road or the foggiest
heathlands was only ever captured on sad nights, in gloom,
where the lone flights of obscure birds would provide a temporary light that I would not otherwise have: I used to enjoy
ornithology. I had more passion for dinosaurs than for most
other things when I was little, but it was not a *practical*
passion. Am I misremembering my past? These aspects of
life are described so glowingly, enviably, I could not aim to
invoke them without sounding artificial, or like a thief.

I remember a keen interest in the natural world as a
buffer to urban encroachment, but I was never a boy scout
or some *Swallows and Amazons* type. I was too weak, physically, and hadn't the fortitude for those pursuits. I took de-

light in nature in sanitised reflections. I memorised the illustrations of wildlife encyclopaedias and extracts from magazines with zeal and depth, but my physical interactions with the world could never extend so far. I was limited by my illness, trapped like a dog in a corner. I sauntered carefully in autumn meadows and wept under trees at the sight of death. From birth I was destined for a future spent in the specialist clinic, and at a young age I was a regular inpatient. And while I kept an earnest interest in nature throughout my adolescence (surely it is still in me somewhere?), I had later to become accustomed to feeling aloof from the naturalist's course. Or any work. Or likely any conventional route or normalcy that could attach me to this ecosystem. I shifted into the mental seat of the sterile urbanite though I still lived in the countryside. I watched the silhouettes of nightjars in the late evening—briefly stumped by their metallic whirring—and spotted spoonbills on marshes; but it was never (save the most gorgeous of limited experiences), the romantic ideal of dancing with wolves, sitting by Walden Pond, or killing squirrels for sustenance. It was eerily distant. My experience of nature and the country, like a veneer I could only glance past, was deeply important to my growth and gratitude despite its aloofness from me.

And I drifted away. I want nature to return to me even if I cannot return to it.

My walks are further restrained to urban jaunts or loitering in local woodlands, if I can walk at all, and while I want to recover something it is not of fleshy naturalism *per se*. Did I have that anyway? I'd not want to recover it due to the fear I earlier described of people loving something too much, and so I feel a guilt by association in loving that thing too. I'd want to recover, rather, and however poorly sketched, an importance of natural place and natural character—even a revelry—that does not resort to the power and jingoistic talk invoked in elections. Not the force of character through threats. Through all of this youthful curiosity, tinged with the scent of hospital linen, I felt pressured to write down notes and ideas and occasionally collate them. Unlike what is conventionally described as awakening a philosophical interest, I had no care for *wonder* for its own sake. I was instead pressured, a little begrudgingly, to convey thoughts rather than go mad, and I picked up some liking for a part of philosophy, or the history of ideas, along the way. I found however that what I wrote, whether theoretical or concrete, always became biographical and at odds with the common demand to be impersonal.

There is a literature of despair that I need to move past but cannot forget. I do not want to assume the pessimistic attitude of Schopenhauer but I cannot forget him, and he is useful anyway. I still see sadness and grief responded to reflexively, and therefore not properly contended with. Memoirs of loss and grief are numerous, and so I risk repetition and boredom. Yet what else am I to do but this therapy that doesn't exceed the possible? Despair needs to be the penultimate word, where the last word is impossible. My entire work amounts to being the diary of a disappointed man, and I recoil equally as I embrace the only perception I can know—hung up with my health and hurt, without any real course to mend things. I at least want to illustrate my wishes, however poorly.

Say I go to the coast. I walk alone or with a friend along a stretch of cold beach, frequent a café, or try an ice-cream despite the crisp air. This is an ordinary thing but one I somehow struggle with. What am I to say of this? At once, there is an immense gratification at the simple, yet also a bitterness—and when I speak of my strange quandary, the subtle differences in a chronically ill life, of how I am not nor ever can be satisfied with myself in a simple setting at the day's end—is it alien to those I say it to?

Or would they articulate similar worries if not so busily engaged in the world of healthy people?

I can try being a flâneur to forget my troubles but it loses charm without company to share or time to write while travelling.

My problem with revelling in the ordinary, no matter what motivation I have to like it more, is that I hold so earnestly, against my desire and my deepest wishes, something cool and sterile and firm about the outside world, which I know is not objectively possible. I think this is verisimilitude—the banal truth of reality. An empty or hopeless world that is correct.

I had, when thinking of ordinary and seemingly simple things, an arrogant stubbornness that was childish, or like that of a curmudgeonly old man. I would see this discord at my remove from things and feel so much despair at what I could never rise above. I would still trouble myself over what was impossible, in events or in my personality, rather than seeing the impossible for what it was and trying at least for what was possible. Nor could I convince myself very easily that nicer things would otherwise be there. I was always *divorced* from basic events, without ever having been married in the first place.

I was so heavy-hearted seeing the world. I despaired as if I were Heraclitus[6] in this most trampled way, and one that felt pretentious and snobbish. I desperately want a love for my friends, to fend off a world that could look like Zapffe's

---

[6] Heraclitus of Ephesus (535–475 BCE), pre-Socratic Greek philosopher, noted as 'the weeping philosopher', sometimes contrasted with Democritus (460–370 BCE), known as 'the laughing philosopher'.

The Last Messiah[7] ... I could hear the cackling laugh of Silenus.[8] It was there so clearly and I wept at it till it hurt my bones. I didn't want that image of the world.

I had to find my summer.

I have a distinct young memory of a spindly tree—preserving its blossom before autumn in rural Suffolk. It was quintessential, an easy subject for painting, and likewise for pretention. I cannot place this in a definite geography, but I remember absently staring at this picturesque tree caught in the biting wind. I was struck by the perseverance of the blossom. It seemed that every year it had to withstand the rain and wind of a dull Britain, as I did, but it fared better. I somehow linked this picture to something, imaginatively, like a child's fairy story or fable, as something I would recover only later to make a literary point about. I stretched it into a metaphor that I dismissed and didn't live by consistently—about our use of and relation to the natural world. Most would fail to really see this tree, but in distinguishable ways. Either *too much* would be read into the beauty of the tree, its artistic value, its *spirit*; false personifications, thus seeing past what is there in material truth—or it would be ignored as a pointless thing, an

---

[7] Peter Wessel Zapffe (1899–1990), Norwegian metaphysician and mountaineer, noted for his philosophically pessimistic and fatalistic view of human existence, inspired by Arthur Schopenhauer (1788–1860). Zappfe's most significant essay, 'The Last Messiah' ('Den sidste Messias'), was published in 1933.

[8] In Greek mythology, Silenus was a companion and tutor to the wine god Dionysus. The Phrygian King Midas was eager to learn from Silenus, and so captured him. When the king asked for his wisdom, Silenus laughed at him and shared his pessimistic philosophy that said it would be better for man to have not been born.

ordinary fixture, not even worth study, where no pretentiousness should be afforded. Yet I want to afford it, I'm urged to, in my own endeavour, in reaction both to those that wouldn't see things and those that would see things too extremely, and so misread the world. This reflects not just our relation to, say, the natural world, but how we relate to illness and sympathy. What we have is the tendency of some to attribute too much significance to things that nevertheless really do have some significance. When people read too much into things, there is a kind of loss due to the addition. On the other hand, people also tend to do the opposite, finding no significance in things that merit more of their attention. In a phenomenology of illness, this very basic point has a lot of power and I don't think it can be overstated. This is, to me, a root cause of the problems which face me. Relatives and friends may read too much into my pain. They might try to help me too much. I don't want to be suffocated with sympathy. At the same time, I deserve some level of sympathy and recognition for what is actually going on with me. It would be one thing if people could take one look at me and understand everything there is to know (i.e. all the relevant information and history which explains my current condition), but that is not the case. People don't know unless I bring it to their attention. This can serve to generate even more confusion if I fail to convey things properly. So then there is the wish to not say anything at all. But staying completely silent, while perhaps preventing me from ever being wrong about anything, almost guarantees that no one will notice the pain I endure. This problem extrapolated into wider concerns certainly gives us some doubt and fear. To be ignorant of simple Nature, an ignorance represented by neglecting something so ordinary as a blossom, means not seeing a world falling to moral or ecological calamity; we overlook destruction, and, in reaction, those distressed by this—too bothered by all that they cannot solve—respond by imposing their own poison.

I see a double-threat in false premises from both sides of an imposed divide: that of obfuscating spiritualism and that of sterile reason. Those that feel too intensely and those motivated by cool disinterest. The romantic sensibility against indifference.

A gulf is enforced between these two positions, but my aim would be to establish a commonality between them. This schism isn't wholly Manichean, that dualistic view of good and evil, but the most worrisome of ideas and people propose that dark and divided scene.

Perhaps the only threat is my own struggle in how to see. But I could not maintain a sort of solipsism and say other perceptions did not align with that which I detested. Perhaps complete apathy or indifference would be a more looming threat, but the self-satisfied, with these opposing paragons, filled me with more fear. I later translated my memory of the blossom into an attitude, held tautly, there for rebuking many misgivings.

This was a dim oppression I saw. It wasn't a specific violence or marked aggression against me that was foreign to me; it was a general despair, a heavy concoction of my own frail body and disease. I could not weigh sufferings against each other as quantities, but I had a prop that my world would build around. My world would still be irritable and grim.

What are the enemies of this oppression? What Nietzsche referred to as *oppression*. I struggle to express myself without sounding puerile. I had the ghastly reflection of the world's terror, and my sad observation, but there lurked beneath, as if I would class it as a nemesis. . . a breed of pride, a taste, force of character, that couldn't just be some lurking bad thing. Something that I would mistake for belonging to detestable causes by not finding my own definitions: by not declaring the fluidity of these words and eliminating their malformed associations with those who used them threateningly. There are virtues we need, disassociated from guises, which we can ineptly choose to best suit us. That make use of tastes that can be easily misused. The last century had this same problem, as did the one before, and my words could seem like some form of moral posturing. As well as being self-evident or common sense. If so, I wouldn't be too fond of it. Posturing morally, especially, is a bit of a dirty thing that doesn't fix much. And as I hope to describe later it is distinct from good moralism.

My attempts to reawaken or rediscover *character* or *pride* are not hung up on bringing back past affectations, nor found in traditionalism—the dead faith of the living that gives tradition a bad name. They would demand a removal of *things* when we harken to past deeds—a situating of persons and contexts. A type of history that while not supernatural is also not bereft of colour. There's too much in this world, I cannot account for it all here, and my personal survival requires ignoring some things and specifying others. I do not want a force of brute, colloquial power, of campaigns expressed in mean slogans— but a natural vigour and love of nature we leave to be mistreated by political fetishists. It is the vigour that makes the blossom withstand rain that becomes the poetic aspiration.

The next set of troubles shows the arduous course of maintaining aspirations when faced with mean opposition.

I am still in part averse to feelings for my home, if not for the feelings of others for their own distant places. There's an envy there, as much as reproach for the most zealous.

Britain has a perfidious history, sometimes not seen at home, yet one I would unfairly hold over myself when I measure my self worth. Again, I was affected too much by the outside to be left alone in finding my own worth. Love for this place can manifest well . . . there is a certain beauty to the woods, the heaths and the coasts that I cannot deny—of their richness and humble glory. There's even that which passes for mountainous terrain. There's a wide selection of people who may as well be noted. But it is easier for this adoration of place to reveal itself in hubris, measuring injustice against injustice, where banal but severe temptations are lost in frustration and abandoned to excess—the blight of violent adorations expressed without temperateness.

I want to show this place love: to refine me, my workings . . . I want the invincible warmth as felt when basking in mild sunshine, the scents of unknown flora and the sounds of early winds—I want to sense these details of the world without the thought that I am succumbing to a cliché, where I need enter another emotional universe to escape feeling embarrassed. I'd not want to be associated with such mockeries that misprint the world. I cannot live in a world unto myself. I need the outside world to be comfortable too, and yet I cannot rely on it so greatly or otherwise delight in upcoming calamity to feel good. I appear stuck. I should learn to be less put-off by the mismanaging of the world by and for others, especially if I half-assedly talk of some Samuel Beckett-tinged *quietism* on occasion.

What I want . . . In the morning, fresh moisture on the ruins; something young on what is ancient. Being somewhere, transient, with an old wisdom that doesn't harken perniciously. And then passes. It's the idea of a past that could be valuable but without exaggeration or false foundation. There lies my imaginative attraction.

There's a point that will recur in the refutation of things: in finding our own comfort, we make alliances with the external and form attachments to the material. Land. Oceans. The Sun. People. And so we should care to better reflect on what *material*, sensual attachments mean.

We begrudge the materialism defined by excessive greed for property and luxury, and we should begrudge those narrow-chested lives, but that is not something we can take as a standing to deny the idea that our baser belongings, and *materials*, are invested in our worth and our memory. More so, people. In the absence of belongings, they may either become even more vital or one may attach less significance to them. You might envy nothing. To lose belongings, especially those hard to replace . . . viscerally affects us and we should be more honest in not denying it. But we pretend to be austere spiritualists when faced with loss, as if we may live on immaterial ideas and hope; and then take that to another place that is further unjust in allowing people to be without mundane and worldly things. It's evident that most of us, myself included, seek attachment and investment in objects—which are lesser forms of investments in people— to help amount to our own being and attest to our own being. And surely the world is too cruel for us to be asked to live *so* modestly? We find little comfort in an internal essence, soul, or whatever you would call it, on its own, *alone*. With no shoulders to stand on. Or belongings imbued with our memories. We are infected by secondary knowledge while we are alone.

If I lost this entire work in the process of its creation I would be distraught and it would be too difficult to replace despite its comparative brevity. It would probably not be repeated—I have a timeframe. The same distress one would have if they put time and bleeding effort into a film or project of work, a belonging, that was then lost. If such art, writing, and other creation was not you (your body and person), it was obviously part of you. It was a material testament of you, to you, something which you looked to in order to prompt memory; something you simply used and spent time with that would be hard to replace. Yet we speak as if things were easy to replace—as if we really did live in a world where such things didn't matter so much, despite our actions, our greed, and our dominant cultural infrastructures.

Person or object—there is diversified pain to such loss. It is cruel to deny that pain by measuring it against others, or, with a rudimentary religiosity—denying the pain of things impetuously as we can do when drunk on ideas or in some bad mood.

Simply: place, items, commodities, are important just as people are important, in their own degree, and we should recognise our frailty in our need for things. If I espouse an ontology and a metaphysics that is rather bare, I also have recourse to sensual moments, but with provisos and conditions. The *aesthetic life* is often not enough, but what of the others? Whether a materialist (I'm not too convinced I am regardless of the above) or the philosophical antithesis, there persists the importance of place. The hollowing and critique of place, one's own place, spiritually or politically, in response to misconceived ideology, requires prudence unless it wants empty results.

Objects, one's background, one's country *et al*, are impressed upon to help us, and may be abused as any idea or anything would be, and it is soon unbeneficial to be critical yet not affirmative. We succumb to puritanical denials of our need for ordinary objects and peoples, and look for inadequate replacements. To face a world of shattered atoms alone? We can recognise gratuitous material greed, obsessive nationalism, and naked hedonism for their failure to ultimately satisfy, but that should not mean a return to an opposite state of self-imposed vagrant humility lacking temperateness or real moderation.

It is obvious that most live in a compromise between the two extremes, but moralisers want to live extremely. The result of their austerity is a critical living but one without even such modest pleasures and attachments as we all deserve. Like recommending thrift to the starving. And what attachments are then inevitably found, instead, are shallow or desperate—and then dangerous in that desperation.

I need some type of materialism. I cannot accept vague spiritualising that denigrates me, tells me I don't need things, must do it all myself, or can, with enough effort, do without the material. Or that I must wholly rely on others for my care. Ultimately, that sort of aimless criticism doesn't help. We live one way and speak in another to try to forestall our mistakes—failing to see that some of how we would live does not merit condemnation, if maybe sympathy, and we wander in our inward paradoxes. I will miss lost objects. I can maybe get over them or replace what is easy to replace. I will lose people and myself. That is a greater loss. If you lose a friend, you lose how your other friends would be with that person—a whole part of them now locked away. That intimate behavior fostered by another presence is now gone. Why do we deny how we are so affected by exterior things? We fail again and again at being insular people, making ourselves only with ourselves. I find most supposed examples of this suspect—only a few persistent people really manage to be so truly austere. What is secondary to us is there, outside, beating, making its own account, and unless we are so meek and confused how would we dismiss what contributes to us? We may have solitude but we also need solidarity.

I speak of *belongings* in my failure to find a better word, and in doing so I am, admittedly, frustratingly vague. I mean when I speak of belongings all those aspects of place included in a person's own identity, and the question of how much one is influenced by exterior things (nation, society, etc.) or by one's own solipsism (personal/intellectual growth and growth in spite of the former). That could include everything from the books you own to how you feel about a town or city—how otherness that is physical contributes to you internally—that I will not simply call *immaterial* influences. I'm holding physicality to be the vital aspect, but I won't reduce it—starkly—to a bland *physicalism*.

I am trying to make a tenuous link between a nuanced idea of physical materialism on the one hand, and how to personally cope with perversions of abstract cultural ideas in ways that are extreme on the other. I have a strong feeling that this whole presentation is philosophically primitive and I am unsure how to word it without a bland appeal to authority. Do I hold an untenable position, too nebulous and unsure? Must we have instead a stable foundation, established and untarnished by living contradictions? I vacillate between my contradictions—both in this specific attachment to my home, and more generally—and it is an ongoing conflict in philosophical position and personal worth, a passionate type of uncertainty, that gives the image of my world.

Why am I so bitter and conflicted that I cannot enjoy, so easily, my physical place? Why am I so uncomfortable? It is all I have—myself in physical place. Or all I can see. I've never had any time for a transcendent or heavenly world to escape to, so less is given to me, in this cooler, indifferent reality. It is then harder going when, without that sort of spirit, we would adopt equally harmful but linear religions and ideological certainties to fill the empty gulf. This mundane world gains a vital aspect, if it is the only one I can have. How am I to find my worth in it without resorting to crude certainties, lies, or a more absolute sort of quietism—or rejection? If your home has a history, even if you do not care for it, it means others will care and therefore impact you: act upon you. And we can't all live like hermits to escape that. I have to contend with this societal fact even if our world is meaningless, or perhaps, because it is—meanings will be perverted by my neighbours and I will need to deal with it. I can't escape into solitude to avoid misused meanings, I can't escape in faith or blissful ignorance, and so I burden myself with this conflict.

Culture will contribute to your survival and character even if you are hardened against words. Again, I cannot so flippantly shake off external influence. Even if I would sometimes want to be without it. This does not mean excess *pride*, but an acceptance of both our natural and national agencies, at any rate the least unjust. I would have statelessness but it is unavailable to me, and it would be a posturing gesture. Denying your own history for so long from an intellectual's armchair starts to erode you, such a broad past affecting the personality perniciously, and so those condemning their own place appeal politically to another that they don't know rather than figuring out how to amend their own. That's the extreme but common reaction to not liking one's own seat.

My struggle to appreciate my home—both politically and philosophically—would not be about any grand diplomatic fix, or historical pride (which has done enough damage). Rather, it is about being given the courtesy to feel quietly comfortable in the place where I have to stay after I've bashed it for so long. If I want to, I can still keep note of what is pernicious. But in the desperation to fix where I live I should try not to stray into worse oppositions where I think an enemy of an enemy is somehow a friend. Not finding 'the grand fix' (or denying its existence) doesn't mean I shouldn't cultivate my own garden and a place where I can feel well—rather than reflecting ineffectually on all the very obvious flaws of Britain.

I will still betray my country before I betray my friend, and I don't *identify* with it in that common way. I just want a measure of what I can realistically do within it, *how* I might contend with living in it alongside its people, and of what isn't really very helpful in admonishing it. Because, realistically, I won't be going anywhere.

The fetishising of history, by friends and enemies alike, shouldn't stop me from finding a personal reprieve in a synthesis between excess patriotism and cultural admonishment. Between a fetish love and an obsessive hate. The problems of exaggerated national pride are obvious; those of national self-disgust contribute to wavering morale when it is needed most in times of crisis, but also are exposed as voices: fine to slag off their own place to the point of death and deny their lineage, while finding allies in those distant to them who'd throw them under the bus without a second thought, and who in their desperate alliances, fail to see more terrible things—sponsored tourists walking obliviously through Ukrainian famine . . .

The profusion of voices can make liking this place—even with its better qualities—feel stale. Its niceties and finer beauties can be lost in files and bookkeeping, in futile argument. Places receive affection from those who do not comprehend them well, or know how to love a place, nature, their home turf, without rudely squandering it and corrupting the possibilities of national allegiance. Places, too, can face a scorn which is unbecoming. To hope for things becomes unwise, while to languish in despair becomes foolish.

I want to return to my home and feel safe on its beaches—unsullied by the misuse of pride.

IN ABUNDANCE: REDUX

The mass profusion of content and paraphernalia in the modern world can work against an idea of appreciation for one's situation. While recanting an old motif, this passage is also an expression of and reflection on modernity: on what modernity does for one's own worth if they are concerned for their own esteem, what trappings and bearings contribute to their self-esteem, and if they want to give a sense of real feeling in their oral history as opposed to a dry re-telling of history (a basic chronology), with little context or situation.

Given that this is supposed to be an indulgent memoir, I am concerned with how I feel with and reflect on the situation I can distinguish—and as the modern world is a slippery beast I'd want to give (as I can, if clumsily) an impression of how its contents affect me.

A new, exponentially increasing abundance of media and infrastructure fashioned from the technologies of present civilisation means we are situated in a disordered place, or at least one that has lost the illusion of order.

The multifariousness of everything means enough pros to living in a new space, but equal cons (something vapidly obvious), and the removal of an idea sometimes seen as ineffectual, even churlish, but something nonetheless important and taken to extremes—which is *novelty*.

This is the essence or the quintessential idea of a place, commodities, people, or oneself, that is too easily perverted by nostalgists, the puritanical, or those who have a false, inept sense of history and what something was supposedly before. If we are to portray in a better light what this essence is, what appreciation for our places should be, then we need to remove from its equation those who misuse words for blunt propagandist motives.

These are fancier words for saying there's too much, and that more and more means less and less. It's not a height of pretension to say that the noise of so many voices can sully a place and hinder a personal connection with it. But we cannot move in rudimentary and idealistic directions in trying to somehow amend these perceived dangers. It is a world of bombardment that would drive one to madness if not for sufficient psychological defences or evasion. Today things happen so fast that a mind struggles to absorb them. Art's capacity to convey begins to fail.

There is neither heightening nor relegation of quality ('*goodness*') in this new content, these cultures. This is not an ethical judgement of the past as somehow better or worse. That is a deeper case than a resolute condemnation of any one period. Too many people condemn the past or discredit the present with easy words, reducing the world to a single formula or a single conspiracy. What should be praised as well as smeared requires more than one explanation. It requires a depth that most would prefer to neglect for their ease.

In modern history there exists the same sort, the same uncertain degree, of quality in the tabloid and the popular as well as in niche or counter cultures: the same indefinite idea of a relatively consistent beauty *and* a steady rate of filth. The gossip was always bad. It is difficult to apply a coherent historical measure to the changes in media, and many would do so far too anachronistically. The artistic quality of cultural artefacts in different eras remains mostly consistent, though not by a formal measure, as to truly measure it would be entering a confused territory of banal subjectivity—a personal aesthetic. Was the media or the catwalk fashion of the 1920s better than that of the 1980s? I will not say, just that I have my own preferences. There have been cultural and technical improvements—that goes without saying—but some things can be said to be worse for more insidious reasons.

When the year 1984 came about, Huxley's *Brave New World*, published over half a century earlier, seemed more prescient than Orwell.[9] What we loved would more likely kill us than what we would rightly hate. So this isn't a question of a boorish politics or empty statistics. These can be seen as improved or diminished by one's biases. We have instead a nebulous question on artfulness and the amount of attention we can afford in different media.

The problem being diagnosed is that of having too much of a *quantity of culture*, a different marketing of culture, and what population growth, overconsumption and overproduction mean for the exposure and portrayal of arts and individuals—not just ethically, but in terms of attention we can afford to give them. What happens when things are faster? What does quantitative growth mean for attention to quality?

What are the cultural implications in a modern world where so many more people have the opportunity to contribute? It can mean that just as many—or more, by numer-

---

[9] Further reading—*Amusing Ourselves to Death: Public Discourse in the Age of Show Business* (1985) by Neil Postman.

ical quantity—fine and wonderful things exist; but by the nature of modern representations, mass media, etc., there is less of a weight and collective status to figures, celebrities, ideas, or places. This can be seen as a loss of *novelty*. Or *Quintessence* (c.f Walter Benjamin).[10]

Modern technologies mean the ability to easily proliferate more of anything (media content), which means the growth of further dishonest content (which is mostly easier to create and propagate) alongside the steady growth of informational means. The lowest denominator in a culture will always be met and so we see a plague of base content as the means of art and creation are democratised.

I don't want the simplest denigration of culture—the modern consumer landscape. No matter how bad some things may be. Fine research and stories are still extant; they are just harder to find in the larger haystack of digitisation—with a broader, diffuse press, and with greater content creation. The creation of algorithmically tailored echo-chambers that can restrict even further what one sees is another story . . . The fabrication of an ideological singularity.

The viewing figures for a television programme during the last century were often higher than for today's most popular shows as there were, at one point, only two or three TV channels (UK), fewer radio stations than now, and a smaller press. They would receive a higher share of the population by default.

More choices mean different centres of attention and often a type of inertia created by the breadth of one's choices—the sheer number of options. There was a different type of celebrity-focus when the means of media production were lacking and differently regulated. More specifically, *public*

---

[10] Walter Benjamin (1892–1940), German Jewish philosopher and essayist.

intellectuals, people of letters, with a reach and influence (fame) could be said to have benefited from their technological regulation—where we now have the proliferation of on-line *pundits*.

Philosophy probably isn't dead and nor will it die, though for no lack of professionalisation's trying; ideas and movements won't die, but well-known and credible *philosophers* are perhaps the casualty of academic trends and the shifts of a wider media culture, with people now cloistered from public appreciation. This (the priority of focus) is what could be missed by us, though we should bar any harking sentimentality. This case, this romantic point in history where we are better occupied with letters or literature, cannot be returned to—and nor should we try to—but there can be a reasonable wish for different attentions.

What was hitherto a majority consideration, a popular TV programme, may now be relegated to a niche interest in the popular world—though its numerical support is still at least present as it has an audience to sate it. But while the numbers may be equal, it does not follow that—proportionally—shows or books or people are given the same fraction of coverage and publicity—and we may see in that a problem for the dissemination of ideas and, more vulnerably, cultural narratives and their stability (both personal and public).

Old media meant products could be widely seen, but products were still confined in their number by technological ceilings, which determined and formed the boundaries of a culture. New media means there are more and more products and far less restriction. This new era of anomie and wider choice will obviously have its harmful effects; though in noting that, and in the same breath, one should not revert to reactionary functionalisms or misplaced traditionalisms that proclaim the decadence of new culture and the need for dreamy returns—ideological or not. The case for the defence of modern *atemporality*, the defence of today, and the supposedly opposing case for rooted old ideas are often equally tragic and unoriginal.

The new millennium gave us not just new cultural tools, but a new climate for culture to be exploited within. A change of priority in what is *celebrity* (often the focal point of how a culture appears) long evolved past our first Byronic conceptions of modern celebrity, and the continuing trend for visuality as prominent and pre-eminent over text (no matter the profusion of new text and podcast) can be seen as a symptom of technological-cum-cultural shift.

Self-evidently, it does not discredit these new tools that they can be put to poor use. Celebrity is something that can be enjoyed and used well. It is not a wholly negative concept (we crave it as much as we reproach it), and we take for granted how the popular figures we venerate are the measure of a culture.

In a culture of technical limitation, a product could be afforded more weight and influence as it was not embedded in so huge a mass of different sources. There's a kind of revolt that disposes of old orders, however terrible, but has no suitable or effective replacements for how to root ourselves (see the civil unrest of May 1968), and engages in an ongoing process of finding out what the hell anything is or should be, that often fails. It would be easy to accept crude demagoguery or some other rashness to save us from uncertainty.

I feel no moral nostalgia for a wet-dream of a past age where quality or morality was superior. That would be spurious and is not what I have in mind. My nostalgia, my harking, shows itself rather as a mild, sometimes throwaway attraction to particular moments, the history of some memory or idea, some person; and instead the feeling of

distinct cultural perceptions, the need for roots but a prudent use of them, descriptions we could still enjoy—not
facile archetypes—while displaced and moving in the mass
of crowds. Instead of lost entirely.

There were always equal wonders and horrors, but our
problem (mine) is our age of the newest visual reporting,
sharing, and useful technologies. I cannot abide Luddism,
technophobia, as an instinctual reaction to cruel societal
changes. Fervent neo-luddites, neo-puritans, are not palatable. *The Anti-Sex League,* all the religious zealots of a secular world . . . they are mistaken in their diagnosis and cruel
judgement of modernity. But there are still things that are
bleak.

With our new, muddled and disorientating *technics
and civilisation,*[11] these sorry sorts who never before
would have have been able to contribute—beyond letters
of complaint—can now be seen and heard everywhere. The
consistent ignorance or unawareness of the public would
have been, with whatever benefits and dangers that has,
restrained. Almost nothing now exists without the invi-
tation for public comment—without a near-instantaneous
(and normally useless) public response. Now one can freely,
with an effortless touch, without mind or tact, violently
say what one impotently thinks when nobody need speak—
more than one ever would have done (as one surely would)
before, sitting at the bar and harmless to the community,
rather than online. This bad talk is obviously not something
I'm immune to either. It doesn't help us. We're still as isolated no matter how well-connected. There's enough space
for constructive work from actual constructive comment as
well as the utterly banal or rude, or even violent, if an author
of an article or some such thing is tactful enough (shaped

---

[11] Further reading—*Technics and Civilization* (1934) by Lewis Mum-
ford.

by an audience's response), but the existence of such near-omnipresent shit accompanying anything—neither functional, critical, nor positive . . . but thoroughly pointless . . .

It may be said that I have a parochial reaction to it (the public) and that I am arrogant in my dismissal of such dismal people. And I sense I have to guard myself against those instincts. They've been given (the general population) the greatest ability in the history of publicity.

There should still not be so much of a barrier to the real questioning of things or growing to be a thoughtful person in discourse regardless of formal education, or lack thereof—though that is a rather common or obvious truth. Our openness is good there. You don't have to be in an ivory tower to see and make change. Though people with qualifications still make ridiculous judgements (we can take John Adams'[12] assurance that many great writers have expressed nonsensical views), now we have the added burden of people with nothing good to say, or nothing to say at all, thinking they are deserving of a place in the discourse rather than learning, and having some modesty, before they think they merit a platform or money for nothing. We used to have less of this self-promotion because there were fewer means of attaining it. There were more confined editorial standards (for better or worse), and people would accept their imposed quietude—if querulously.

I am trying to describe the problems of a modern culture without either glorification or a crude dissatisfaction when we reflect on the obtuseness of modernity and publicity. In our modern world we get the celebrities and the intellectuals we deserve.

Our pundits could at least make a minor effort in their thought and calculation rather than spend empty words in

---

[12] John Adams (1735–1826), American statesman, writer, Founding Father and second president of the United States.

more of a performance than a substantive characterisation. Though that's perhaps a hope too far . . . Fetishims and mass media don't often allow a reflective intellectual pace—with the constant need for debate and spectacle. Could we even escape the society of the spectacle?

With the contemporary world comes mass saturation. Slowing down to reflect goes awry when surrounded by zooming things. And I want something reflective over something so hurried. It is in some way a primitive wish. A quickened culture, as well as one of mass quantity, neither reflects nor understands itself very well. It fools itself into thinking it must move so very quickly, move away from history (good or bad) or act as its illusory culmination, that it will be safe as it is, or even believe that its racing will lead to success and a new world order; not realising the extent to which people hold ignoble grudges from their history—or crudely against the new world—nor seeing the strength of an enemy that might dislike their rushing. An *enemy* who themselves may be corrupt in their reactionary tastes. Nobody on any side of these perceived, multifarious divides takes too much care.

Even if one is now more capable of gathering information, said information will not have the time or space to be ruminated on, and it is in constant danger of being overtaken again and again by something new. To be slow and pensive is not some unprogressive antonym to needed change or progress. It is a mistake of sensibility to think that opposing a hyperbolic rush means opposing a necessary direction of moral or societal evolution. How is it controversial to wish to be more considerate and careful with how and where we step? The idea that a more contemplative speed could be contentious or even condemned as *conservative*—and against our interests—is the mistake of hurried implementations, some themselves reactionary or opposed to true reform, that have fallen prey to an anger that cannot cope with the world's injustices sustainably; or cope with them in a way that only unravels them with the short-term throwing of babies out with bath water à la heedless violence and ideological pipe dreams. Nevertheless, there is still a problem in what can look like perpetual doubt and performative questioning rather than actionable assertion—of tone and posture while Rome burns. One needs the balance between reasonable self-contemplation and action that isn't ineffective or counter-productive.

It may be of some relief that no idea is so dominant in culture—now so diffuse and unfocussed— as it once was in past centuries, where ideas would have stake and direction but be horrifically acted on and applied. But what now *does* have a stake but some tepid lack of direction or soulless consumerism? A previous intellectual elitism, however reproachful, is gone; now impossible, as the tools of a culture have exceeded old boundaries. Few are good at predicting the future. People may deserve this ability to speak so very widely and excessively—I am one of these suffering people and in assessing the swamp of modernity I cannot be a patronising voice. But the age of old media and its fewer voices did have a slender advantage, arguably, in how it was constricted and delimited. Even then there were our well-known and much written-upon cultural homogenisations and those plenteous causes of alienation. Now? A sad truth is that one is often more motivated by things rarely heard than by a ubiquitous cry of injustice heard every day from every outlet. That becomes tedious. The abundance of our life, again, causes some restriction.

Democratisation of media and the free rein of anyone to contribute does not clarify it seems, nor make good the maddening crowd, and especially in an exponentially growing world that needs to be quieter if it is to be even temporarily understood. Let's not get started on the faux-revolutionary hopes of *accelerationism*. There's no stopping, so it will hasten into nothing or doom, not realising what it is doing; no self-awareness, no reprieve, bereft of its institutions.

Replaying the above, the old world was no better in quality—its voices were just as terrible and at times just as pleasant—but it had less quantity and that meant something different. Its quaint elitism, the confines of media and communicative channels, meant that what was distasteful was at least corralled by established limitations. Opened up, we have a rough abundance. And there's no going back. The best hope would be to maintain an (intellectual) honesty in our openness.

Press will be perverted by mass.

THE FAILURES OF DISCOURSE

In philosophical and political discourse a climate has likely always been present where failing to show group membership or ratify an abstract and even conflicting message under an agreed name, even in the most compatible way, will prompt a pointed dismissal. Not declassing to partisanship engages the fury of the partisan.

I cannot consign myself to strict systems. I'm not of the right temperament for systems. And I cannot abide schemes.

To systematise the world is to kill it. My rough sympathy for the artist above the (technical) philosopher or narrative partisan comes through. Not any grand one, but one characterised by its views on the banal. I do not want to explain everything, nor could I. If you grandly calculate the world, spiritually or materially, under an encompassing and singular system, a pinnacle method, and say 'here, there is the truth', you commit yourself to a lie: narrowly ordering what is in all likelihood ultimately, unbreakably, nebulous and unknowable to you.

This is not to say that there are, then, no truths, that all views are legitimised in the blandest way in which you could understand philosophical relativism. It doesn't become the straw-man of William James'[13] style of multi-

---

[13] William James (1842–1910), American philosopher and psychologist.

viewed pragmatism or a crude drawing of badly and barely understood postmodern theory.

There is not, here, an absence of narratives; proclaiming an absence of narratives is still narratological. Yet there is still a wish to remove the most *certain and acting* of narratives. It is that which has the conceit of grand order, certitude and satisfaction, over doubt, over relativity, and then confidently enacts its purposes and explanations, that is far more harmful, frightening, and practical than even a self-defeating or apathetic scepticism. Of course, '. . . The worst are full of passionate intensity.' It has been said before: the latter (scepticism) is to be feared in its own place, but political motives most often present the greater terror of certainty in ideology, rather than caution—wherever and whatever it is. This does not mean—in response—neutrality, or lack of commitment, or complacency.

This tone is often more attractive to a pessimistic sensibility than to a strident political one. An ethics of experience, only loosely translated to philosophy, is less attractive to those who want a stage to justify themselves or for definite action.

It portrays a *wishy-washy* effect, as if self-doubt was untenable—uncertain being frightens them, and sadly, it is hard to fathom that as committed and responsible when it instead takes the impressionist's approach of seeing multiple angles, is committed to knowing things honestly and as it can by regular revisions, and takes care to not step callously into a mess it knows little about.

When and if it does take steps it will have, it hopes, the requisite understanding rather than some dim reading that pretends it is more. It is the avoidance of (as the Germans say) being *inkonsequent* (inconsistent).

As to the aforementioned *failures of discourse*, we may first reflect briefly on this author's epistemological and ethical state. Bluntly, I can recognise hypocrisies and failed attempts at intricacy in my thought; and I can see what I think is ignored in many stricter appliers of theory . . . which is the muddledness and mess of one's thought. To recognise above all one's own incongruity and that of the wider world is not a puerile misdirection. Systematic workings are lacking in most thought—a lack of coherence and comprehensiveness which is still attested to as if it did exist in all spheres. The act of thinking means, again, rethinking and then re-thinking some more. Are most of our readings of theory not shoddy, as we pin down labels and allegiances? We name what we do not understand. As if we were not hypocrites. I fail to order myself to a *cause* easily, apart from an obstinacy in my critique of ideologies aspiring to totalism.

Of hard-learned restraint that isn't stuck, I have no true polished view to offer. I could never say that would be available or viable to me. I cannot seize the world. It always slips away. I need then, to confusedly try to accept the mess of things.

I am weary of the world and unable to carry out the best and most conscientious of philosophical investigations—which leave me cold anyway. The most I could attain would be an accord of feeling for my fellow humans, and to reject so many prosaic injustices wrought by those colours and leagues in their most virulent anger; and, too, in their ignorant complacencies.

I cannot make history. Others will do that. I can at least say that what is pestilent exists. One can spot falsehoods if not the most final of *truths*.

The modest hero, instead of feeling vanity, recognises their own inability to be and do what they wish as a course to seeing what they *can* do. Personal, meagre heroisms— a real, non-colloquial happiness that is far harder than heroism—come from ordinary people out of a simple, even simplistic decency. Courage. I dream of that.

> One of the symbols that I have used most frequently in my novels, essays, and lectures over a period of decades is a bridge that does not exist but materialises bit by bit under the feet of someone who musters the courage to step over the abyss. The bridge may never reach the other shoreline, and that far shore probably does not even exist. The evolving but never complete person on the bridge that extends only so far as his courage does, and thus never far enough, has become the hero and antihero of all of my books.
>
> —Manès Sperber, *The Unheeded Warning 1918–1933*

To see or accept this lack of polish is often seen as *spineless*. It is lacking conviction, some would say, as they prefer absolute certainty and perfect solutions (perfect ends) even dull and dim-witted. They can't accept an unfrocked priest and will prefer even a fanatic to a reasonable doubter who changes clubs. They can't seem to have just a lightness of touch.

They want the grand plan laid out for them that wrangles all of history and actualisation beneath it, proving its end, when what is this really? This decisive stratagem . . . but a hopeful divination and a myth on all sides? On the want of so much definitiveness . . . I've never seen much cohesion even in the greatest of minds, far above me or anyone I'd be privileged to know. I'm fed up with canned dismissals among those who won't recognise themselves, of all stripes and descriptions, underneath their ideal facades.

> Objectivity is a subject's delusion that observing can be done without him. Involving objectivity is abrogating responsibility—hence its popularity.
>
> —Heinz von Foerster

Real progress . . . comes in learning you were wrong all along, and all alone.

The ubiquitous and deluded objectivists, those so allied to absolutism, ever indulgent, exacerbate my struggle for self-acceptance. They wear down on everyone. They stop us from being content. Where can one avoid them?

Retort: why care about what others think? This has always been easy to suggest—recurrent enough to enter cliché and eventually meaninglessness. I'm not sure what to reply besides that, yes, I do care what is thought. I care what is thought because that builds me as much as my own essence, as no sure intra-personal originality really exists. I am repeating myself. I can't be completely reasonable. It is impossible to be, and indeed what is real, really *real*, is irrational. Or arational. My reason built upon irrationalities. It is Pascal's note of the heart's reasons of which the mind would be ignorant. You still have appetites for things and even avowed hermits would care somewhat for the outside world. They cared enough to avoid it—and I can't be a hermit. So I have to care.

How to broadly justify my mindful weariness: I'll look at what I can see (as narrow as my scope is) of the nature of knowledge, of what we can say beyond basic empirical observations. That is to say, abstract thoughts, judgements on observation. Great framers of definitions reconstruct the world through their own indulgences rather than any certain outside measure. My own objection is caused by their relationship to objectivity and intersubjectivity, and how far they think they can take their impotent minds. There are political ends based on those more abstract forms now made certain simply by their insistence. Having been a bit too critical of our own capacities and dismissing the thought of heavenly possibilities, there are still stories, ones to love: human stories bound by time. We still live as what is little and precious within mere and ungoverned history, not the cosmos. The universe probably doesn't have a story. I still—at least—have the truth of humanity without ultimate meanings or calculation.

In rejecting one possibility of human thought or action, one does not need to reach for its supposed opposite. The assumption that one does makes me tired. So this sort of unpolishedness and lack of certainty in thought is not to dismiss something—Reason—entirely. Just as above one doesn't reject truth. Quite the opposite—if one rejects a Hegelian rationalism (or politicised Hegelianism), or the extent of the archetypal philosopher's psychical power unaffected by bodily ill, that is not, then, a rejection of the power of reason and rationality. It is to take into account the scope of reason, practically, and by what we may really do with ourselves. I guess my labouring over this is due to accusations that have been levelled at me. In saying I don't approve of something, I'm left open to the accusation that I reject reason itself and am the worst of anarchists.

There's an elementary place for rational treatises and a simpler logic for the everyday: tactics and planning, organisation and argument, for sciences and for various procedures, and to reject reason would be stupid. I've never done that. Far from it. But what I'm speaking about is unreasonableness, not pure unreason.

I don't suffer from some relativistic subjectivism or an anarchic kind of irrationalism. Be rigorous enough in the application of reason and you'll reach epistemic limits, but I'm not so fully Kierkegaardian as to go beyond reason when it cannot go any further, or leave behind logic when all grasps at it slip. Reason becomes useless, though I don't think there's much beyond it—and it is itself, built on irreconcilable feats and necessary complacencies. There's no truly stable ground and that can obviously cause some unease. No world beyond the aesthetic is hard to accept and dissatisfying. But that is all I cope with, and to show more of what is unreasonable . . . we see that wider abstractions rarely translate fluidly to lived-in philosophies of-the-day. Nor do quotes and inspirational posters perform well.

We may have logics and rationales to overcome this condition of modernity, *more and more*, of feeling lost, etc. Yet how clearly these are implemented is variable, perpetually variable, where real reason goes amiss, and I have no sound measure for how I am more a product of impulse than I am of exact reason. This is not an endorsement of this reflexiveness, but an observation of its strength above my intellect.

With this thought of irrationality it is bemusing that I'd be occupied with others who will, in the last analysis, be impervious to argument and have for the most part made up their minds. But disengaging from these people would be a more reasonable position, recognising a type of futility, and I'm again not *so* reasonable. I'm obviously pessimistic about political possibility, so what actually is possible?

Let's try to be more specific. In the past I have suffered from an intemperateness of tone. Maybe not in writing, as tone is harder to define and I am more eloquent in writing, but in discourse *per se* and how I would act and carry myself.

I have the audacity to think I have matured a bit, so what does this mean for *tone* in how one wishes to reasonably convey something of yourself—or in trying to get something across to someone? I also have my own propaganda to show.

In a well-intentioned tone of disapproval for people's ideas a lot is said that would not merit conversion to better positions—or establish understanding for anyone involved.

I'm expressing here my aversion to debate in its inadequacy. I can abhor the results of intelligible certainties, of many a definition, but the stylistic choices made in expressing dismissals often only appeal, correctively, to those whose position is already akin to one's own, one's own choir, or those on the fence—and would only make the targets of one's scorn indignant. Targets of reproach need harder demonstrations to be *converted*, if you even have the influence to do that. The more vapid and ineffective types of protest against various injustices work similarly where the fever and hysteria of one's understandable suffering negates practical, real measures to overcome or remedy an unjust authority.

The inadequacy of debate and discourse can lead the committed to perilous cliffs. I can give yet another example of this harmful sentiment, which also shows my bias against ideas still sadly extant (despite how comforted we otherwise seem). They show the failures of a common discourse.

There is a basic and reasonable position: the spirit of rebellion can reveal the evident. It can reveal solidarity with the oppressed and the imperatives of sympathy. Revolutionaries of history, of the most violent variety, then betray this spirit in their firm devotion to an idealised history. So convinced of their goals they can become, like those powers before them—and with clear consciences—tyrants and oppressors. And true justice is not achieved.

This is an easy thing to say. It has been said enough. There is little fruitful discussion with these zealous people, and they express the failure of protest in brutal form—when instead we should want protests and revolutions that are in fact effective. Where their arguments fail, they take up arms and shoot themselves too.

It is maybe a relief that many would-be terrorists can recant their actions at the last minute, even after extensive planning, as they search themselves and ask their God if they really need to do this. That one last doubt dawning on them with the brutality of what they must do, that would offend their own sensibilities prior to radicalisation, can start to dig at them. That final doubt in dogma before the most cruel and needless of acts can redeem them. It may be of some bemusement that even radical Islamists could be, at that extreme, more shaken to doubt and to find another path—or a more peaceful one within their existing frame—than the comfortable bourgeois set firm in their attractions listing quotidian Marxism, or their support for the Tory party . . .

There is a binary perception of a pure, united political opposition to something seen as equally united in its own brand of fervour. From the date of its inception (our poor memories of the French Revolution) real unity on any *side*, for what sides we can distinguish through some parameter, most simply as *right* or *left*, was always betrayed by ringing hollow: a shallow account of anything.

Unity was always rare as one side always had ten other fissures—and to dismiss one political framework does not mean being tied to one or two opposed positions or not accepting at least the most basic agreed terms of a dichotomy pertaining to particular places—if not universally. Frameworks, especially political, inadequate graphs and spectrum diagrams outmoded for decades yet still routinely attested to can be dismissed while standing in any corner. There are always contradictions to note in one's philosophical and political subscriptions, and in what one is named as externally. Linguistic confusion finds itself most abundant where discourse is explicitly political. The history of our political vocabulary shows gross misappropriation and feeble cataloguing, but for fear of repeating myself, or Aron, Koestler, *et al* (re: various sources on the datedness of political measure-

ments), I'll quieten on the point of rejecting many definitions and wishing to teach differences.

Today's world demonstrates a sustained appetite for violent or grossly obstinate ideologies (whether capitalist, fascist, or communist), or for the fervour of violent overthrow
at all costs, even if without the influence of previous generations, and a conviction that any co-operation or intermedi-
ation means death. It shows as well an equally sustained appetite for powers to remain even if they are cruel. We never
got a *post-ideological* turn.

There is on many a side in pursuit of their goals an absolute damning of individuals when one still needs imperfect
allies; we are thoroughly incapable by ourselves. The world
for these people is still Manichean rather than confusing,
multifarious and diffused; they see themselves in their consciences and their theory as almost perfect or obvious, when
the world and what answers we can have are neither perfect
nor always obvious. How does one achieve a nuanced reciprocity with minds that are so fanatically partisan?

There are opposing extremes that perform the same acts
of dethronement for different ends. Can one bother to discuss such things with either *totalitarian twin*? Can you convince Lysenkoists?[14] Is this medicine for the dead?

These thankfully moribund but nonetheless vocal personalities, revolutionary or counter-revolutionary, often excuse any pragmatic or far-extending chance—at remedying
the ills they see by slow increment and preserving them-

---

[14] Lysenkoism, named for Russian botanist Trofim Denisovich Lysenko (Трофи́м Дени́сович Лысе́нко), was a political doctrine in Joseph
Stalin's Soviet Union that mandated that all biological research con-
ducted in the USSR conform to a modified Lamarckian evolutionary
theory. The underlying appeal was that it promised a distinct idea
of biology based on a view of life that was consistent with the view
of human nature insisted upon by Marxist-Leninist dogma. Lysenko
was, nonetheless, a thorough fraud—attacking the legitimacy of science for political reasons.

selves, monument, justice, their own legitimacy, and life; if they would want to do that anyway, which many seem not to be so interested in.

Destruction at any cost for a prophetic end, one that is not possible, excludes the possibility of useful creation, the truer possibilities of slow modification, and real sustainability. Nor is a reserved, old establishment really a sustainable or stable locus. Short-term battle may merit the taking up of arms and the consequent destruction—I'm not advocating a resigned refusal to fight, but the long drag of ideological discourse doesn't warrant unfettered barbarism, random anger, wanton death or all of one's violent, forceful means.

Is this battle against fanatical ideas, against ideologies, that of the last century? Are we, in a very simple use of the phrase, in some new, post-ideological era? Perhaps battles in the new arena of politics and war—that I won't hope to pertinently and correctly dissect—don't have these same historical stakes: the press of *Cold War*, the awful struggle of interwar and postwar crimes, Hitlereans and certified Stalinists (or both their *fellow travellers* and other respective, assorted attendants) . . . today's atmosphere is cloudier and has its histories based on newer varieties of grudge, different techno-cultural hallmarks, with men and women and others who breathe different air—and only the foolhardy will say with such sure and definitive tones what the state of the union is.

Contesting emptily, faltering in assertion, ideals of justice pursued with bad ideas: it seems that lots of voices—even if these voices are confined to shouting at walls—are still afraid of admitting their intellectual insecurity (one I must honestly admit but try not to flaunt or patronise), they offer the world their certain solitude but with sad condescension, and are reluctant to present their diagnosis of world affairs, themselves, the direction of history, or a study of past influences . . . as *unsure.*

Those who could really give a good and detailed account of history or sociological directions, military rationales, cultural grievances, are more often quieter, subtler, obscure and reserved sorts who in pronouncing conclusions will inevitably be shaded and aware of the varied complications of analysis.

Rather than Ockham's razor, those hearing these notes from the rarer and closeted, and not receiving the simplest of headline answers, will prefer the vivisection of Ockham's chainsaw. Not a simpler world, but a simplistic one. The review that so many are eager for both in the editorial office and in comfortable living rooms: an answer.

A column must surmise all the world—everything must be said. A summary is reacted to so fiercely and confidently by so many typists of all descriptions that one becomes as upset as they are suspicious. A moderation these people are surely capable of in the cases of their private activities disappears when faced with anything external to them. Moral outrage is easy—true moralism is hard.

One could simply dismiss these efforts as intellectual dishonesty. No matter the creed or allegiance.

This earnest desire for the easiest ordering of things seems to manifest in all ages, in varying ways as a lack of a particular modesty while feigning weariness; lacking a wiser maturity. There are those who appear polite and modest while still suffering from the same conceit noted above.

The nucleus of this straightforward, simplified divining of basic order has its worst reflections in our multiple radicalisms. If I was more studious and less lazy or fatigued, I'd invoke Miguel de Unamuno and his Ethic of Doubt.[15]

---

[15] Further reading—*Tragic Sense of Life* (1912) by Miguel de Unamuno.

How we forge the basis of an ethics more prudently, and free of dogma, should reflect the honesty we would wish for in striving for good discourse, quality thinking, and remaining just while living in the ontological unknown. It is not pallid scepticism stuck in its own contentiousness but the astute and forwarding use of possible nihilism (in a rejection of it that doesn't forget its ground), seeing the problems of scepticism, and using itself to work around them while not forgetting the importance of that doubt in curbing cocksure thought and vanity.

Few historical figures agree with the idea that we function on the basis of a pure reason, instead concurring with Samuel Johnson's description of 'the perplexity of contending passions'.

We have passionate minds that misuse passion. They don't practice a particular moderation, nor temper moderation itself, and in their unfocussed anger they shift the cruelties of the world, not seeing where it is going or what it is becoming. Hubristic tendencies root their way into the more egregious examples of partisan action; no matter on which periphery, those wishing to persist in intellectual consistency and honesty, and the elimination of lies (where '*truth*' is a fishy thing), may do better to step back and consider what anyone, including themselves, is really doing. Practice *wu-wei*, even; my wish is simply to have myself, or others that would bother me, conduct themselves honestly, conscious of the difficulties of intellectual responsibility, before they take steps carelessly. Truth isn't reached by jumping off the cliff.

A saving grace as much as a bane is the willingness of most to live calmly, in querulous gratification, despite injustices. If more people were moved to action by their dreams and desires there would be more crime and injustice. Tories are only half-competent: imagine if they were wholly competent. This pains me, as there's no wish to keep up the particular conservatisms that propagate all the usual social injustices—our current violence is just as awful as one that wishes to change things over upholding the unjust (I have no time for the Right). But considering the brutality of death I have had to restrain my stimulating dreams of change that is called for with pressing emotion, and recognise the debt and cost of usurpation that would be beyond me. The mollification (mitigation) of injustice should come before a staunch and awkward march to an idealised revolution, and especially one founded on false sciences.

Today's victims as tomorrow's executioners is an obvious and banal objection, yet the *realistic* and *practical* actors, wanting captive minds and futures, opposed to being morally condemned, see who has discredited them as, at best, detached from reality and from supposed *vital interests*. In a better light the *moral side* is seen more admirably as literary, maybe artful, but still denigrated as some vague humanism somehow abandoning the necessary harshness of real politics. It would not occur to these *so realistic* of people that even airy, fluttery words could actually represent an unwavering stance.

Little is done, maybe, if one isn't murdering the pets and relatives of an awful leadership: but what is achieved by replacement? Does extremism succeed in providing real justice its most famous forms? Has one only, actually, betrayed real revolution for a lofty cause that is out of reach? I feel banal in saying this, as if it were all said and done and I am just a parrot.

One is not resigned to the unjustifiable if they neglect to murder people.

You are still intransigent against what is terrible: you still deny it a discourse: when you must you still prepare for war: and when the most important of changes is possible . . . it is best done when one has the tact, resources, prescience and responsibility which would help one to do it correctly—rather than with the impatience that makes things worse in the long run—a perpetual *agon* unresolved. Risks are necessary. Removing the lulls of bureaucracy or fuddled heads in show business, fostering innovations, requires taking risks. But that is different to the kind of political risks—crimes in fact—preached by idealogues. Many of those indignant orders of violence are called for in the name of idealising rather than a primary feeling of desperation or a way of real progress. The risks wanted by outsiders from a position of seeking rectification are often different to the risks wanted by those really living within something (re: the ideas of many intellectuals and militants compared to their *subjects*, everyday working people; etc.).

Most cannot enact sweeping change. I likely cannot in any great way change minds or force movements. I do hope that some bright spark would bring about more attentive work in facing environmental woe. Our opponents are stronger than we think and we need to act tactically and more astutely. For institutions to be fruitful, they need time to both define their function and justify their existence. We cannot make new lives overnight.

There is no doubt that things need to be reformed, changed, demolished or upended, and destruction may seem an easy way to beget rapid change. But it is a change that is not often properly targeted, tactful, or one with much foresight into how it may preserve a greater quality of life, or achieve real justice in our lives. Destruction can be romantically attractive and it surely has its place—but it is something that needs to be considered more skilfully if it is to be worth it. Despite its aesthetic appeal, destruction is not always as radical as it seems. It is easy. Again, it can certainly have good use and real justification, yet it can quickly become reckless and distracted. It will, often and inevitably, become just as corrupt, and abusive as a cruel power already in place. What we want instead is a path to real change that would last. I should make clear that I am not objecting to riotous reactions to prosaic injustices—righteous anger at racial injustice, for example. Which I share. Rather, I object to ideology developed from a variety of political extremes, often opposing, that take the idea of destruction somewhere else, in an unjust way and not fortuitously. I am equally opposed to those who stand more for 'order' than they do for justice, and who in their conservatism are persistently cruel, violent, dismissive, and destructive of community, ecology, or simply a good living for more of us. There are various people opposed to this, still, who speak of justice but do not deliver it—and their violence, differently motivated, amounts to a similar barbarity. Conservatives aren't very good at preserving the light of the world, and I direct most of my ire against them—the excess of capitalism and imperialism, and then the further reaches of fascism. People closer to me, in their wish to fight injustice, still aren't the best in their practices at providing that goodness, lessening our suffering, or being prosperous. And their failures are more troubling to consider than those who are simply, blatantly, evil. The failures of our friends are worse than the failures of our enemies.

Places with history have felt within them all that has been said within, and cannot easily be replaced. Sense Miłosz's peculiar dissatisfaction with a desert California compared to an expansive Lithuanian history[16] . . . It takes some time to live. Life needs to be thought on. Nor is much

[16] Czesław Miłosz (1911–2004), Polish-American poet and diplomat, in 1960 was offered a position as a lecturer at the University of California at Berkeley. He had described how the newness of California perhaps contributed to his feeling of being lost or more uneasy when compared to being back in Poland or Lithuania.

that is artful really done under that which cannot create new things after a fiery disposal.

A truer rebellion has a paradox. It needs order—or a decent sense of stability. It should not reinstate what is terrible. A politics, not new, of *limits* against injustice. Mediation. Against those most desperate of transgressions. The most rampant type of demolition (of old orders) also works against any idea of bourgeoning support for a cause, as one's only respect will be through fear: and there's little worse respect than that. Nor is it lasting.

Imagine leaving only charcoal to defend . . . We forget . . . that much of revolution has always been an illusion. Especially in our history. There are detestable powers, things that need to be removed, and renovated, but how are we to really mend the world? As if we could?

> To make a good omelette it is not enough to break thousands of eggs, and the value of a cook is not judged, I believe, by the number of broken eggshells. If the artistic cooks of our time upset more baskets of eggs than they intended, the omelette of civilisation may never again come out right, and art may never resuscitate. Barbarism is never temporary.
>
> —Albert Camus, 'Create Dangerously', lecture on December 14, 1957 at the University of Uppsala in Sweden

Razing the ground does not give a pristine opportunity to rebuild, because most are frankly incapable of that. The actors have little consistency, time, cleverness or resource. No time to cover the interval between myth and reality and no moral high ground. There is no real idea of how to properly replace regimes, and more commonly in those states of absolute disposal a void of power and a scramble by anxious and enthused souls with little wisdom or intelligence. It is a questionable idea that they are supporting the governance

of moral history—a notion of true progress that would somehow justify their impositions.

> The so-called dialectic of social history results from
> the transformation of reality into an idea. Each
> régime is sharply defined, and a unique principle is
> ascribed to it: the principle of capitalism is opposed
> to that of feudalism or that of socialism. Finally, it
> is suggested that régimes are contradictory and that
> the transition from one to another is comparable to
> the transition from thesis to antithesis. This is to
> commit a double error.
>
> Régimes are different and not contradictory, and the
> so-called intermediary forms are more frequent and
> more durable than the pure forms. Supposing the
> principle of capitalism to be connected to feudalism
> as 'nothingness' is to 'being' or Spinozism to Carte-
> sianism, there is nothing to guarantee that the acci-
> dental determinism will fulfil this intelligible neces-
> sity. Supposing that socialism reconciles feudalism
> and capitalism as 'becoming' reconciles 'being' and
> 'nothingness', the advent of the synthesis is not pre-
> dictable in the same way as a nuclear explosion or the
> trade cycle.
>
> On the plane of events there is no automatic selec-
> tion which conforms with our moral requirements.
>
> —Raymond Aron, *The Opium of The Intellectuals*

I am only making a cautious note, reluctantly, disheartened at the longer, unsatisfying results of idealised change. I
am anxious to stress and always repeat that some upheaval
is surely a thing to pursue, where we are truly justified to
fight things and do so with full resistance. The story we
can fail to heed, in our justified revolt, in the heat of our
desperation—in favour of reactionary or revolutionary or te-
diously moderatist ideals—is yet again our basic vulnerability and failure. Can our political realities only ever be unsat-

isfying? I am unfortunately, on most days, a fatalist. I hope that you can do better.

Without real justification for what one would fancifully wish to impose, there's little cogent rational or ethical backing for those abrupt ideologies that betray revolt: caliphate, counter-revolutionary romanticism or revolutionary rationalism, the *end of history* . . .

Sad experience has inoculated me against wanton death or extremism for any cause, neither justified nor achievable by fair means, and most *causes* of that so historic ilk are dreams—more nightmares—promising much and delivering little. Social causes worth dying for are not so vindictive. One should not accept definite models and utopias, or be seduced by parables. We don't have those heavens.

To use Sperber's phrase: 'Mark this carefully: we stormed heaven not that we might live there but to show all mankind, *ad oculis*, that heaven is empty.'

A hard message to accept without resignation.

In the need for change people can do better than dream. There are enough dreamers in the world to call for necessary change, but there are few reasonable people to guide us in a practicable direction in an imperfect world and by imperfect means: the only means and answers available to us. Ideologies of perfection are always contrary to psychology, to Dostoyevsky's 'real interests'. Always working against better interests. Posterity may, with some hope, frown upon those writers and artists so absorbed by their agony that they seek solace and uplift through a spiritual *'cure'*, a *cure* in cool diagnosis, in historical prophecy, rather than have their anguish made live, dramatically, as a testament for future generations in their deliberations. Change regarding the most awful injustices happens, change is needed, renovation is possible, and rapid change often occurs. But when it is real (or *good*, and not transient or at risk of a quick reactionary reversal) it is slower than we want, or need, or if it is fast—and yet stands firm—it stands thanks to better planning, calculated by more astute or prescient strategy. The weight of bad things is a lot, and much theorising has gone into how revolutionary change would be automatic or even scientific, inevitable. Among these dreams is some nobility, yet all I am expressing is caution against Icarus. Healthier people detached from real weight can more easily posture about optimistic change. It may be better to act against injustice out of duty rather than hope—and not forget the vulnerable and weak who so often end up as collateral damage.

Greater minds than mine have better exposed the self-subversion of fanatical devotion and a reaction to authority that is frenetic and untamed.

I've maintained already, pessimistically, that many will still be impervious to argument. But what can be done to create a sympathy for one's own position, or to convince the undecided? Anger can name an injustice, but at its furthest reaches it begets disorder, not changed convictions. I am never very angry, in the conventional sense, at those most massive of political horrors. I am thoroughly upset by them. To be focused and upset works differently from an unfocused anger. Anger can be fine for a while, but it cannot last forever if we want to prosper. And it soon becomes poisonous to the self.

I have a blurry memoir of author bell hooks[17] speaking of the chance for anger to be empowering instead of destructive—where the destructive or toxic nature of anger

---

[17] Gloria Jean Watkins, better known by her pen name bell hooks, American author and activist.

comes too easily. Managing to direct anger in an uplifting way and not have it be corrosive is difficult and rarer than we would wish. It's much easier for anger to exist without strategy or astuteness, without a tactician's aim. I can be angry, often, but I don't want to react to injustice only to exacerbate it. I just want better anger: emotions directed cogently.

I would have to learn a sense of understanding for how something adverse, even horrific, can come about in our minds and in our practices if I want to confront it.

Most fail at giving even a proper label to a rival with such a poor grasp of political vocabulary. If I cannot grasp what and how my opposition is, and academically consider their own logic—however primitive it may be—then there is little chance of my being able to resolutely and justifiably condemn them. I may prefer more privacy, now, than to readily engage myself against the incorrect, and of course I cannot kill or convert them. The only possibility available to me, given my limitation, is to maybe stop others, friends, from falling into traps by finding them early. Insofar as one's rival hasn't reached a limit of no return from their darkness, discourse with someone you can still hope for needs to be done with a higher standard, legitimately, if it is to be done.

There are some patent evils, puerile evils, from which many cannot be recovered.

As such I find little reason to shout at them, and measures to counter such fanaticism are things I am not, physically, able to take part in whatever my wishes. I then have the privilege to live quietly. I am so tired of argument against what is obviously dark and monstrous, at pointing out the same things again and again to someone who will not listen anyway.

I give up on the fanatics. You may have better luck.

In argumentation, anyway, I should be more prudent if I would want to convince anyone of anything (especially anything partisan) beyond briefly moving them by impulse and emotional responses. They apply deeper motives to violence, do not care for argument, and prefer to raze things completely where they find them unjust.

I can only suggest that there are no best choices, no definitive solutions—only the next best thing. The least bad thing. To scrap everything so thoroughly doesn't mean anything good will come out of the waste, and history seems to vindicate me (or those others who would say the same thing better than I).

Those most moved by outburst will already be aligned with you; where those who are a real threat and who may consider changing their minds will often not be moved by your passion, reflexively irked, rather, by your perceived rudeness, and instead, if at all, moved only by something clear and which they could comprehend according to their own sympathies. It means to be insidious if you really wish to *convince*.

All this wariness and equivocation on political possibility, the denials of our ability to really do much, the talk of caution about great and grand ideas, is informed from the position of being disabled. It is not bad or wrong at all to realise that disability is an intrinsic part of one's person, and it being a limiting factor isn't something to be ashamed of. A sense that we are more limited than we really want to be, and certainly lack some control, is troubling for many—but it is telling that the most ambitious and hopeful among us are eugenicists. These life-deniers and those who want for so much can live without even acknowledging the existence of true limitations—they are ashamed of them.

Again, I'm simply pessimistic about justice being achieved, with the strength and brutality of the enemy.

With how little others care, with the weight of injustice being so heavy. Especially with disability justice, with the sustained and persistent cruelty enacted upon us, with all the backward steps, it is little surprise that one might not think bigger things are possible, and that our best, real, or even our only hope would be some mild reform. This pessimism is more controversial or harder for others to accept than apparently radical measures. Don't dare be miserable. Don't make the *ableds* uncomfortable. Elaborate ideas are proposed—that we might really do things, making the impossible possible, as if they don't know how bad things really are.

I want the best change in the world. I don't tolerate the brutish and short life. Forgive my weariness, I am awfully tired.

Knowing that our reach is less than we want is not bad— it doesn't make us lesser people to suggest we aren't so able. We can still pursue greater things, but it's best to not neglect our vulnerability. Indeed, vulnerability recognises popular falsehoods, and may make us more true.

PEOPLE OF RESPONSIBILITY

I have a hard time accepting my world with its setting of priorities, but self-acceptance, if not actualisation, means coping with what is external too, and unfortunately it is hard to live at an uncaring remove from the world no matter how tempting. I am repeating myself. Despite what the meditative may wish to say . . . you cannot forget the world very easily, and to be engaged with the world means something nuanced, a shaded expression, for which we require different depths to our discourse.

It is hard to express this illustration of myself without being circumlocutory. It amounts to tracing an entire history of personal thought that would be beyond my capability to express. I want to show my love for people and their impetus for my growth, the hard-learned direction of my reading and evaluation of ideas, but I cannot spell out the biographies of people in pedantic detail. The purpose of this section would simply be 'Here, these are people I like. I like what they say', as a reflection of my interests. Which is cheap, but my expedience may be justified with further reading. John Ruskin wrote in Exercise VI of his *The Elements of Drawing*, in his guidance on how to draw a tree. . . 'Do not take any trouble about the little twigs, which look like a confused network or mist; leave them out, drawing only the main branches as far as you can see them distinctly.' I don't feel the need to focus intently on too many twigs.

I covet an idea of moral responsibility—one which is mistaken (both broadly and semantically in some languages) with a type of full engagement, purest ideology, at any cost: with action but not with consideration, nor deliberation. There's the imperative to speak on demand, to be (categorically) a general intellect rather than—preferably—a discrete intellect. Caustic ambitions are valued over the thought of not crossing certain lines, and a need for things so powerfully that it becomes all well and fine to endorse certain crimes. I need something against that. I shout: No.

With no restriction there is unlimited slavery.

The rebellious no is not simply a bland proposition, solely of fighting the *quo*: kicking against the pricks, the bastards . . . the spirit of that still holds ground, but to say no in this way is also a rejection of moral apathy and of the brutality of political realisms—in their respective reactions to egregious atrocity, or meaninglessness. It is a rejection of and revulsion towards becoming a prick, or tyrant. Harder to articulate well and harder to grasp with a rational head . . . how to maintain this moral responsibility even in the face of an external world that lacks a justification we truly grasp. To hold upstanding morale without faking, without pretending that it has stable grounds and solid building foundations. Even if it invokes and uses old ways. One can use the good of a God without God, one can see void and not succumb to obtuse nihilism. Our world hitherto was not as solid as we pretended.

We can pluck morality almost from nothing, snubbing the mystical or rational bases that wear masks of certitude conjured to help us feel grounded, and that are hard to live by. Many find this hard to justify, if we need to do that. There is a defence: if one bases all their behaviour so consciously on a dogmatism that is broken, if they do not sin due to the fear of Hell, it is to the honour and benefit of the human species that among us are those who would not be so defiantly bound to solid bases. Those who are so ferociously tied to such cannot easily act like undaunted stoics in a new world of shattered atoms. That most do not desist from good action when they cease to believe in old things—in formulae—is to some advantage. One can count on it that people will invent new reasons for their behaviour: the stuff beneath ideas, the awkward steps of rationale, will save them. If one has held so firmly to dogma, the dismantling of previous orders will produce a great sense of loss. To be reflexive can be more advantageous—reflexive people need not be anarchic or unprincipled. Virtue is not based on dogma, but dogma upon virtue. The better sorts can hold firm and create.

Assuming this responsibility in the face of these dilemmas, against the actively violent, against fanaticism, presses on the heart. It can become a madness. In other words it is a rejection of certain metaphysical notions used more broadly than they could be. Notions used as epistemic justifications for societal ends. A rejection that might seem trite, even—if I lay some small authority to Wittgenstein (forgetting his epistemological wild goose chase) I may at least place myself under his monument.[18] The preoccupation with the above discourse is dismissed by academia as unfashionable, and yet academia fails to dissect the reasons why academics may forget the fogginess of their motivations.

---

[18] Ludwig Wittgenstein (1889–1951), Austrian philosopher. Referenced here in particular for his rejection of metaphysics. It could be said, while I am admiring or sympathetic to Wittgenstein, that his philosophical project was fundamentally a proverbial 'wild goose chase'.

On the use of principles: I am humbled by those many varied, intelligent sorts I can admire even while I disagree with them. There are far more eloquent Gaullists, as well as communists and *communisants*—a conventional West and those of other disparate and opposed ideals than I . . . that will forever be of an openness and creativity beyond my own restricted self. And as is evident I dilly-dally between people in my condemnations. Yet scrupulous thought and great ability—while fostering a knowledge or accumulation of attendant information—can lack wisdom and intuition.

Polyglots and professors will still be subject to moral darkness. They can still commit rape and murder. So what conclusion do I take from this?

I think, at least, that rigour and semantic purism should be secondary to morality or humility. Not that it is unimportant to be rigorous—certainly not—but we need to be studious in a better (or the correct) way. There are many for whom rigour is an excuse for an impoverished morality—a stunted emotional growth. I reject those who 'learn to predict a fire with unerring precision. Then burn the house down to fulfil the prediction.'[19]

Some modern sophists, of the last century and now, demand a reduction of feeling and conscience in the name of what they think is a greater intelligibility. They want to order the murky No Man's Land of decisions, the bad outcomes of good intentions, good done by doing shit; they want it all simply and consequentially ordered. Men of great integrity still commit crimes. They react to evils by exacerbating them. They augment injustice—showing frenetic anger rather than clearer courses of antidote besides wild

[19] From the poem 'Child of Europe' (1946) by Czesław Miłosz.

outrage—not realising that what is best is mostly impossible. They reject such rough moralising as useless and impractical. They ordain, by dirty means, practice that does not redeem us from *agon* in the long or short term.

So practical, so efficient, so easily hoisted with their own petard.

How can I further illustrate the responsibility I hope for—a particular one—by peopled example? In comparison to many others explaining themselves I am neither dense nor opaque regarding what and with whom I identify my character. I just wish to take some care with it; because you say you are one thing and are connoted quickly and instantly with a perceived opposition, and I am a weaselly man who cannot abide that bluntness. I would think it callous and shallow to be able to say what I am so comfortably—picking some available preset costume from the comic store and saying 'yes, this commodity is me'. Easy self-description doesn't portray much depth, and is often a scary sight in those so strident in their opinions. It is always an ongoing, rethinking process that accords me my self-description. And I am still left unsure of it. A stranger to thyself.

Rather than write a complicated treatise, which would take more time and patience than I have, I will substantiate myself anxiously by attesting to the authority of past intellects. I can claim some complimentary allegiance to a list of people to shine a light on my own weary conduct. There's a feebleness to it but also a necessary convenience. As if our own worth was not also found in the roles of others? You write to yourself in the mirror of others. What is secondary cannot not be relinquished from my throat. This is the use of intellectual history. There are people who in their way, in their time, were preoccupied with *a century of crimes*. They are perhaps the best examples (as men and women of letters) of those who did not fall to violent decadence. Neither did they fall to any vacuous pacifism—the quality of honesty reflected in the better judgements available in their time.

The list is chosen, too, for political and indeed passionate reasons: Hannah Arendt, Raymond Aron, Albert Camus, René Char, Jean Grenier, Arthur Koestler, Czesław Miłosz, George Orwell, Boris Pasternak, Ignazio Silone, Manès Sperber, Simone Weil[20] . . . Let's not write out a litany of biographies but grasp at the crux of my adherence.

All these people held something similarly, politically or morally, while their obvious differences go without saying. The commonality of these late writers, some of whom have brought me the greatest joy, was an awareness of our bur-

---

[20] Raymond Aron (1905–1983), French philosopher and sociologist.

Albert Camus (1913–1960), French author and journalist.

René Char (1907–1988), French poet and member of the French Resistance.

Jean Grenier (1898–1971), French philosopher and writer.

Arthur Koestler (1905–1983), Hungarian-British author and journalist.

Czesław Miłosz (1911–2004), Polish-American poet and diplomat.

George Orwell (1903–1950), English novelist and essayist.

Boris Pasternak (1890–1960), Russian poet, novelist, and literary translator.

Ignazio Silone (1900–1978), Italian novelist and political leader.

Manès Sperber (1905–1984), Austrian-French novelist, essayist and psychologist.

Simone Weil (1909–1943), French philosopher, mystic, and political activist.

dens and an antidote to overreaction, as well as underreaction, against moral and political confrontationism.

One should not appropriate their testimonies but merely disseminate them. There is a moral need to bring the suffering experiences of the past into the present, for reasons of awareness, rather than subsuming individual suffering into one's own contemporary, anachronistic goals under narratives of progress and systematised history.

I am not so much an *écrivain engagé*, though my reasons for dissemination are not mere personal therapy. I am stuck somewhere between the desired practice of a self-soothing quietism and the public need for the artist.

Why do I need a list of people? Is it not a pallid thing, almost lifeless, without the detail and pattern required to really speak of a theory of things? I am not here for that. I cannot comprehend or give anyone theory—in any comprehensive way, at least. I come up short, but when I speak of these people I do not do so blandly.

They are not just a recent history of grim events and advances.

I have always needed people (even strangers), the sensual world and the unwomanly face of war to give me my personal history—a history of idea and social biography, of scent and touch. I could not have my measly excuse for history just be some list of events and purposes. I need the words of men and women that I can know intimately. To see the faults of our historical players in context.

To situate these people more specifically in their own experience, my wish is for an illustration of those more unorthodox members of Resistance, additionally, (Jacques Ellul,[21] *et al*) who endured as voices of conscience while they were swamped from all angles by a desire for unfettered

---

[21] Jacques Ellul (1912–1994), French philosopher and author of *Propaganda: The Formation of Men's Attitudes* (1965/1973)

vengeance that turned in on itself, and a Cold War variety of materialism and polarity—consumerism, and the proposed antithesis likewise. The difficulty of this political stance in that time, untied to this or that simpler loyalty, represents an admirable philosophical persuasion I can dream to emulate.

Others, such as Jean-Paul Sartre—still an open and creative intellect—enjoyed a greater influence, yet in the merry company of fellow travellers 'dispensed absinthe morality' through the Left Bank and a revolutionary spirit of the times that often thought in bland binaries, and betrayed true revolt. They were monologists and polemicists and not self-doubting. They were too sure of what they had misread. The vices of capital, the ding of the cash register, still accompanied their contrary sentiments and defiant ideas.

These aforesaid outliers numbered among those intellectuals who did not lose their way during the mid-20th century to either fascist extremism, tribal nationalism, communism, or plain self-importance—and in so doing courted unpopularity and isolation. Their failure to ratify an easy in-group membership caused them grief—attacks from all sides and even from supposed friends. Regardless of that they were not withdrawn, isolated aesthetes. To be engaged in French and European politics is given a higher importance in longstanding tradition— the fallout from 1789— and in recent intellectual history those particular people, remaining independent and responsible, presented a warning to those around them about how they might stray too far. There is political engagement, and then there is responsible, informed engagement.

I choose these people carefully, for I could recite a copious number of literary figures to consume and emulate, but I am here attaching a certain moral to the story. They represent a type of confrontation to recent events, vindicated more in later years than in their contemporary settings. Again, they are intimates for me, even at a distance in time.

I am also indebted to the late Tony Judt,[22] who helped further rouse in me this engrossed appreciation of the recent history of ideas. A history of causes. As something biographically specific, beyond a broader philosophical investigation, not in abstractions, I became enamoured with these acclaimed outsiders of the last century and sensed a nervous proximity to them, an accordance—in part through tinted-glasses (as I could easily romanticise an already mythologised era)—and a kind of studied devotion to individuals that was applicable, practical, and tangible to me and my life unlike so many other theorists I was inclined towards.

The choices I make on who to disseminate, recommend, and repeat in my own breath somehow, in my own way of thinking, take a confused course. I want to diagnose it but not coolly. I am less drawn, with exceptions, to philosophical tracts from *Anglophone* sources even though I would be forced to encounter those sources by living with them.

I still take Beckett's quietism, and minimalism, as something important and to perhaps embody, and prefer some poetry and novels from my home (Dickens, Forster, Larkin, Orwell, and indeed if it is in my native tongue, of course I will find it easier), but these are exceptions and comprise

---

[22] Further reading of Tony Judt.

Postwar: A History of Europe Since 1945. (2005).

Ill Fares the Land (2010).

The Burden of Responsibility: Blum, Camus, Aron, and the French Twentieth Century (1998).

The Memory Chalet (2010)

Thinking the Twentieth Century (2012).

When the Facts Change: Essays, 1995–2010. (2015).

a more poignant, sentimental attraction. Of philosophy formally (of my more active influences), I was drawn more to the continent and to certain exiled, less popular persons who fought against something, against many things, and who were later exonerated by events (the testimonies of Solzhenitsyn, Leszek Kołakowski,[23] etc.). It was in a specific interwar and postwar history of ideas, written by figures opposed to so many different dogmatisms, that I saw my peculiar fancy. It was as if these people were part of a reasonable fable. I couldn't pretend, as so many would, to be isolated on my island only separated by twenty miles of sea from land with which it has long been intertwined.

My favourite works were almost always foreign. *La Peste* made me weepy, and I would guess that this allowed me to appreciate those distant others as much as those in my immediate geographical proximity. I am still suspicious of those who dislike their own soil too much, in favour of another, but that's already been said. My attachment to English literature and language does not need to be justified. It just is. I live it as it is identified in my being, the place where I have had my growth and physical experiences.

Is my solidarity, then, with wider European sources not so much organic but intellectual? Maybe it is both, if I could be so viscerally affected by lands I am unknown to, holding no direct ancestry to my knowledge; and even if there was that . . . I have never cared too much for familial history—more for myself in my present, selfishly; I always feared ancestry because of its misuse and prefer worldly ideas to old parochial allegiances. But I'm unable to be so cultured and worldly due to my own impediments. Places alien to me, places I will never be able to visit, have brought me more

---

[23] Aleksandr Solzhenitsyn (1918–2008), Russian novelist and historian.

Leszek Kołakowski (1927–2009), Polish philosopher and historian of ideas.

joy than the village I happen to live in. It could be suggested that a projection of love onto a foreign entity made up for the inadequacies of what was immediate to me.

In any event this solidarity is preferential, shaking one's hand across the sea, and not something tinged with a supernatural history, reserved for believers, that I cannot access. I have no love for nationalism, though I cannot claim a spirit of universal cosmopolitanism either, even if I'd like to. Frontiers do exist, but are temporary. I was ascribed the literature of my own milieu simply by being here, tied to it, no matter my reservations and despite the force of my individualism. I attained an idea of my own identity from people elsewhere after simply looking, and through a longer process of characterisation and rethinking.

Those people, and the sore questions they pose, give me a disorganised thesis of responsibility. A shadow of a theory. It won't so soon replace old narratives or fix a new mess, but it may well help me. They, in the eyes of this humble author, are the best to emulate and keep as mindful friends.

We can grow from their outside aid. A haphazard growth of contrarian rejections, valuable assertions, and pity, gave me these varied and idealised inspirations both specific and eclectic. I hold that there is worth inside other things, but I should take care not to misprint those things.

These figures are chosen, studiously, because, as I said once, I value modern voices more than ancient ones, but this position has some nebulous depth that could be missed.

I can read the ancients and there is some flavour, but I have more sympathy for people closer to me, in time, in culture, in shared activities, and in the undeniable element of modern celebrity idolatry I cannot really challenge. It means that by biographical detail these men and women lived in a time within living memory and can maybe better serve, being closer to us, our modern functions and kinships. Or mine.

One cannot so surely pluck Epicurus or Aurelius from history and functionally apply them. I appreciate them, but we can be too quick to apply ancient thought to modern times. Indeed, many commentators are frozen in their time and place. Their concerns are, in part, no more; and we can only extrapolate from their reasoning and experience insofar as we understand what they were dealing with in their time. There is only so much timelessness to principle and we have a temporal priority.

Maybe I also react to ugly dismissals of people without reading and the suspect nature of the canon . . . Even the last century has moved quickly. I may be trying to indulgently describe a liking of something I need not explain. It is just important that I like something.

I needed voices that are closer to me. Warnings and ways of coping with my own life. It is far-fetched to expect modern politics to take Montaigne or de Tocqueville as primary driving influences, cited directly in manifestos and policy, and I find little use for philosophers as political participants, most of whom 'fall down the well'.[24] Individual growth may be the more prudent course, but again I cannot be so easy with where I stake my claims. These listed persons did good at least, committed good, and I see a modern nobility, warts and all, that is still humble and measured.

With my condition I am hypocritically restricted, in fragile conflict, to armchair politics; to questions of personal con-

---

[24] Reference to Thales of Miletus, c.624/623–548/545 BC, Greek mathematician, astronomer, and pre-Socratic philosopher.

science over and above the rules of a party where I have no leverage or presence. I offer words rather than actions. My actions become, whether I like it or not, confined to myself.

A public intellect, an activist, distraught over public emergencies while confident and comfortable in private arenas, I am not. I am more conscious of and preoccupied with an individual and personal morality than of the finer details of politicking, in which I am neither adept nor confident. Yet I am not a complete egoist, nor set against collectives—this is what the responsibility I'm attempting to describe illustrates. When we are so committed to being politically engaged, if we see politics as omnipresent and above one's person, we can forget that charity begins at home, to maintain an insular respect. And we forget to question our own dogmatism. It is maybe a popular succession to these aforementioned people that I dreamily long for, with some pretentiousness—a long-shot in the world of modern saturation. The lack of personal conscience, replaced by a public one, and widespread acts of reductionism make it harder to make the world a comfortable place for kinder sensibilities. I don't often enjoy the conflicts of literature and they wear on my mind, already worn enough. I wince at the thought that I am sanctimonious—interested in a literature of both cure and poison. The string of issues that impede my capacity for adoration, for comfort, of where I'm from, for people in basic livings, makes me wish for an unexplored life.

I want this easier comfort, both as a participant in wider affairs and personally, that is hindered by my discerning sight and others' corruption. I envy the crowds and their liberty that I can so bluntly disdain.

And in my envy I cannot help but note their callous disregard for the consequences of their unexamined behaviour and the harm it can do. How blissful it must be to live blithely, without much care or responsibility for others . . . Some of us are left dead in their wake, when our lives are so precarious and more fragile. I hold on to this precarious responsibility from others I note above, but it's desperate. I pay some homage to people, note their mistakes, I wish for better readings of things and to reduce harm. Surely others can attest to that too, but again I am limited. I accept this limitation, any intellectual or physical limitation, I don't feel much need to prove myself or strive for so much. If it's all just hot air, at least I may be warmed by it.

WHY I WRITE, WHAT I WOULD WRITE

Much of my preceding bibliography comprised a maddened accounting of other people, of those whom I deemed worthy of proposing and propagating. This does too, but lately I have embraced an uneven form of collations, *literary* prose over technical intricacy, as a way to compensate for my lack of formal capabilities.

With the accounting of others I knew vaguely that I had little to say that had not already been said, and this put me in an impotent position.

One could easily conclude that there is no need to write anything, at least technically philosophical, and add to the clutter of an already saturated world.

All I could really say that would be deserving of evaluation and critique will have been done in a style and class far above my capacity. Some years ago, this produced a lazy, ignoble effort on my part—citing too directly from sources with some brief amendment or commentary, before or after declaring my approval or disapproval. Biographical details, historical descriptions—these were things that I both dutifully and duplicitously decided could be borrowed from other sources, with summary edits, and I wanted to reaffirm and restate facts as if 'for the record', still giving the most basic credit and due, and adding my own weak conclusions.

Why did I need to repeat in my own words something already described with more precision?

It was as if I'd take a thesaurus and my meagre ingenuity, and replay what had already been said plainly and well . . . A lot of authorship seems to be like this. I wrote enough of my own rubbish, though not intentionally, just as one breathes, to supplement what I was fond of—and at least the experience gave practical editorial lessons that are still being learnt. I do not regret this path, acknowledging the youthful drive of it (and as has been said—physical and pathological weaknesses may give one some leeway), though I do wish retrospectively that I was not so lethargic in my aim to retell particular stories. I still am now, and this book could be a lot longer than it is.

In the past I had a more rigid, seemingly common adherence to a type of positivism and a literal readings of things I'd now not approve of, and if I interrogate myself I see these qualities are now highly mitigated if not fully removed. When you reread your past there's going to be obvious recoil at what you wrote. I am irritated by plain mistakes, style and syntax, but simultaneously there has to be an acceptance of the time, age, and the place I was in that fostered those words. I still scarcely know how to write.

As well as this recording of others came a sly, suggested, though not directly expressed motive as to why and what I would write had I the time. The acknowledgment of this set of reasons became clearer with repetition and re-reading. While there is some air of formality to my writing, I managed to reveal without a full understanding—that only came later—that these projects were therapeutic and personal exercises, excuses for prose and brief essays, wrapped in a thin cellophane of philosophical academicism. They were private journals before I had an idea of myself as a pamphleteer. The repeated 'cf. Montaigne' finally meant something—to write 'for oneself' came more lucidly into view than a dim idea of aesthetic justification. A devoted writer should find a new start in each book, though there is an obvious referential quality to all that I do.

I was never good with stylistic consistency, with structure, and I'm prone to tangential writing and style over substance. Seduced by bells and whistles. I still struggle to judge all but the most egregious examples of poor writing. In style and language one would be attracted more to the aesthetics of words, but often to the negative extent of giving 'solidity to pure wind',[25] so common in philosophy, where a writer tries to sound far more profound through the words and phrases they pick. I can look back and sigh at style, but it was something to learn from. And it would be sentimental to try to purge my vocabulary of all these wordy additions that come with time and reading experience. Undoubtedly the act of publishing my work became an egocentric experiment and reflection on my philosophical and literary growth, in an oddly public display, not confined to private journals or empty blogging.

My first attraction in text was to a type of scholasticism (a caricature of it), where I wanted to inflect my self-indulgence into a type of professionalism. I soon realised this was a mistake and with hindsight it is more obvious, again, that everything I was doing was a personal project—more memoirist than philosopher.

Though my error was clear to me, I was conflicted, as I still retained the peculiar taste for formality despite my technique, my personality, basic editorial mistakes, eccentric structure, and I was ultimately confused—and still am—as to what I was doing.

I had to speak from my gut and from my flesh. To that associated, and less in wildly abstract terms. I should say definitively that I am, in essence, a haphazard diarist over anything else.

---

[25] George Orwell, from 'Politics and the English Language' (1946).

There is more recently in my thought and writing a preoccupation with moralism (not in the derisive English sense—'to moralise'—but more in the French sense considering a long tradition of saint-like *'moralistes'*, distinguished from the *public intellectual* by their own sense of private disquiet). That is to say, to be a *moraliste* but not a *moraliser* of polarising rhetoric and violent enthusiasms . . . we need to make this important distinction. It is to have in some part an ambiguity most would disavow; they want so much *engagement*, politically, and expediently, but lack the responsibility to be thoughtful or even correct, and they write a *tract* which is less favourable than showing a basic temperateness or awareness. I don't offer *lessons*; reasons for teleological *advance* (others can give those), we have a countenance with wrongdoings and the slim possibilities available to us.

I have already noted the authors I have admired for what they've reflected, and the following simply continues that interest. There have been efforts by the likes of G.E.M. Anscombe, Hannah Arendt, Bernard Williams, etc. of modern *moral* philosophy—whether formal or informal—and this seems neglected beyond, in methodical form, trying to judiciously reflect all sides in answer to medical issues and ethical action (abortion, euthanasia, etc.), and even outdated *duties*, and not so much an overview of the *meaning of morality and psychology* in a secular age, still holding modernist rejections and certitudes, that has been touched on yet still dismissed for political expediency, rebirthing and transplanting an ethics of old, and sceptical fashions. In short, it more often focuses on avoiding basic conflicts of interest and legalism rather than defining and dissecting a good moralism—and learning from the experiences of the vulnerable.

The subject of real morality is still left, eventually, to the pious. And that does us a disservice. When moral philosophy is most commonly considered it is either professionalised and academic—and so neither public nor influential—or when it is public it amounts to platitudes or the kind of desultory *self-help* none will (or should) take too seriously; or is, again, left to those haughty moralisers with an arrogance we would not wish to suffer under. Worse, eugenics at the expense of the ill and disabled is still more popular than it should be.

Ethics, and then morality, carry on almost through sheer force of will, or ignorance, faith, and is tied to social mores that we don't dare look into very deeply—we live reflexively even when we say we construct ourselves on solid bases or in the work of a religious author. If all we really have, at the base of a universe sieved through all deduction, is faith in our stock . . . then countenancing this is important, not passé, and we can still maintain standards and limits refuting those more pallid scepticisms, as well as fanaticisms. We can still have some measure of Reason in Hell.

This type of *accounting*, not a systematising which we must not have, a modern scope upon the order of things, has, to support its claim, a modest moralism, using the efforts of those invoked above.

Those to see as shoulders to stand upon and live up to in good faith.

And yet this idea of a contemporary morality, and a broader ethics—in an absent or indifferent age that is unable to return to past dogmas and struggles to preserve its moral sense under nihilism without leading to extremes or false *cures* . . . This is becoming a boorish topic for me, in my fixation on it, in my dissatisfaction with all the hard-worked results and intricate attempts at the renewal of past things. It is still a shtick I can't dismiss. What I want, in a Camusian sense, is a *modern tragedy* as my reflection. One which can lament tragedy after its diagnosis and not be deluded by exaggerated visions of the past or future. Faiths cannot claim a monopoly on what we see, even loosely, as virtues; nor can they claim to be the only type of restorative fiction and function that makes it possible for us to deal with our terror.

If I were to write (with more doting effort) on this most weighty of subjects, thoroughly and with diligence, I would need something different from the usual *formality*. I still attest to both my own worth and the worth of outside things through external voices. This means I am far less original. I am less meditative, then, meaning less absorbed in my own confidence to come up with such things on my own. I have no War I lived through, no long age of experiences, but only my own mangled set of feelings as I face a nearer doom than my peers and friends. If I do attempt formal work I would reproach the confines of *scholastic* formality; the professionalisation that suppresses thought more than any outside dogma—let alone making something unenjoyable or even impossible to read . . . To write on this is to not write so plainly and miserably on events. Nor so rigidly. Nor in firm *reports*. Nor any defined set of directives or demands or decrees and dogmas and whatever other doctrines one could use to embolden and employ themselves. My home is not just some pile of professional bricks. It is my meagre being.

We are told by a vocal lot that we must uphold our thoughts originally, but of course we have hypocrisy and if you dare mention others you must detail every tiny aspect of bibliography. My thought was thought by another? We know this. Am I to care? I could adhere to that kind of stringency, but I am not cut out for it. I crave—vapidly, but also in a dearest sense—external feelings, themselves chaotic, disseminated to approve and colour my own mismanaged soul. As much as my own unhealthy experience. . . my sourcing of others is not part of scholarly tradition.

To speak of morality is to speak of a messy identity, and while I may only be able to write of dreary self-feeling, and not some grand tome on other people's, I must, I think, speak of myself. But with vital assurances. That is what I would write. I must name these assurances in a project I'll not be able to complete—sifting through many names and ideas, lists and personalities, in a desperate quest for them; an outline of my own modern ethic may be surmised (if indeed it must be corralled and narrowed-down) in four parts: Aron, Camus, Unamuno, Weil.

Again, this is a dissemination, not an appropriation. If I had the energy I would assemble a comprehensive treatise, of a sort of grandiloquent modern moral guidance (not a formal decree or creed, of course), founded mostly on the convictions and sentiments of these fine examples, and a study of their biographical and intellectual histories.

I select Aron for a particularly commendable rigour and thoroughness to historical overview: a modest search for basic truths or the elimination of lies: and a prescience in light of subsequent events. Here I want to invoke an Aronian realism, not *realpolitik*—the idea of what one should do within the limits of what one can do. And, too, a conscience in how to react effectively, not just emotionally or violently. Aron's *Memoirs* reflect such modest diligence and care.

In this sketch of a project Albert Camus and Simone Weil attend to further details in conduct, behaviour and justice; and Unamuno helps reflect the stark, frightening prospect of founding an ethic in full knowledge of the lack of 'solid foundations',[26] unable to so simply forget the worrying implications of extreme scepticism—or in other

---

[26] Unamuno: '. . . what I wish to establish is that uncertainty, doubt, perpetual wrestling with the mystery of our final destiny, mental de-

words of nihilism; nowadays very much saturated by over-definition.

This is the delicate, conflicted process of thoroughly rejecting the cold indifference that nihilism, or anomie, begets to the uninitiated while not neglecting its existence. Begrudging nihilists are still anti-nihilists. The term nihilism is throwaway as well as too precisely designated, but it vaguely expresses a truth—that of doubt. Want to eliminate doubt? Stop existing.

Other figures could perform this task and fill or replace the roles of those I've elected to represent particular behaviours—or hold similar theses—but for brevity and by preference I will attempt to illustrate the histories and circumstances of these figures, to situate them, and then extract their personalities to demonstrate something of my own ethic/aesthetic while avoiding anachronism. A personal story attempting to poke at a higher profession. While belonging to the last century they are present enough in our atomic and technological malaise. Our issues. Current trends and interests, etc.

None of these figures could be taken wholly to help explain my own convictions. I cannot embody them fully and it would be wrong to do so. The required godlessness, a blasphemy, of Camus outweighs the Christian sense of Weil or Unamuno—but the latter's encounter with the failure of strict rationalism to vindicate God, and then ethics, is important as a grounds for the requisite epistemology and is associated with similar premises found elsewhere with myself and those of varied allegiances (Camus, Nietzsche, Kierkegaard, Lev Shestov, *et al*: not so alike in themselves but facing similar issues). And each figure provides in their

spair, and the lack of any solid and stable dogmatic foundation may be the basis of an ethic.'—from *Tragic Sense of Life* (1912) own limited way the significance of irreconcilability in our concern with the choices we can make.

What is incongruous has power, and what is congruous is determined within the limits of subject boundaries, so where the study of logic and empirical fact can be grappled with, it must be informed by an awareness of limitations that does not exceed itself or usurp its own seat by over-insistence. This substantive project would be a detailed system of argumentation and theory aided, without shame, by past authorities, just as those authorities would have undertaken. This is my day dream.

I have a long track record of writing on Albert Camus. It is easy to be aware of Camus, sadly coloured of fame, but he is someone I actually cared to learn about more extensively, and I daresay more accurately, rather than settling for a banal and commonplace reading. I found comfort in Camus especially as I discovered literature and philosophy during hospital admissions as a teenager. I came across many obvious names and relatable works, and published my own reflections, but it was always Camus who offered me the most kinship and an aspirational image of what I could be were I less morbid, while also retaining my ontological sensibilities.

I read everything I could find by him. His notebooks, private letters, articles, essays, plays, novels . . . and I found such affinity in a decent, open-hearted man who could serve as a rough image of the *moral responsibility* I want. I fear idealising him though, and he knew full well his personal missteps. I am saddened by those who claim to *understand* someone after reading just one thing, as if the sordid life of a

painter could be known entirely by one vista . . . Camus offered the only literature I could truly say I loved. He showed
an ethic and spirit, a journalistic integrity, truth over expedience, standing against death. I don't care how facetious
that is, or how so many could misuse it, mislabelling and
misnaming him; I know there is much that is considered
better in both quantity and quality, but he seemed the least
wrongheaded, to me. What was well-known and accessible
was reasonable, much else misunderstood, but once you got
through it you could see it had the right tone. I once tried to
dislike all his work and his life as some outside experiment
and could only recoil at the terrible attitude it would be to
hate such things. As such he stands correct.

By biographical coincidence, I too was a goalkeeper in
my youth, and had to quit sports due to my ever-declining
health. It was personal demands as well as literary (and
philosophical) that created my image of a familiar aspiration, a familiar friend. An inspiration I could always return
to. Camus, in his ideal form, represented an emotional place
where I wanted to be, if perhaps less adulterous, even if
my reading was somehow wrong, but I could never seem
to reach that place.

A reiteration: beyond a diagnosis of the world as *absurd*,
I favour his sensibility, not necessarily for any typical *intellectual rigour* but for the right sort of comprehensive and
measured sensitivity to his times. The right ethic in the face
of cold injustice—a rejection of messianism, of utopianism,
or much else of anything that seeks to justify the violation
of humanity for abstract projects. That is not a pacifism, and
indeed it does fight and revolt precisely against cruelties—
it is a wish not to lower oneself to dogmatic extremes in
the name of the false or unjustifiable. It is a revolt that says
no to death and murder. This wasn't, obviously, some airy

and clichéd thing. It looked cautiously at the lowliness of nihilistic possibility.

Camus was scornful of pridefulness, the long history of pride in horizontal religions such as freemarket capitalism or Marxism: a pride that is not a reflection of virtues, but a single encompassing vice of murder often affirmed as necessary for various *causes*. It is better to note limits above that of wild possibilities—and stand against those of disparate stripes who under the hijacked name of political *realism* order the bloody sacrifice, surpassing the borders of decency, whether this mind is conservative or revolutionary . . . I want to countermand claims of his time, that persist to this day, that while Camus can be respected for his distinctive and brave moral standing, his quality as a writer, his commitment and responsibility, and the feeling given in his works, his philosophising specifically and technically was puerile: in the words of Raymond Aron. Aron later gave more praise to the writing of Camus, the man himself, his journalism and wartime record, as well as agreeing, reasonably, with the sentiments of *L'Homme révolté* in his own *L'Opium des intellectuels*. But he pointed specifically and briefly to a regular criticism of the man in his (lack of) technical—scholarly—ability with the requisites of drearily formal or academic philosophy. He simply wasn't all that thorough and could contradict himself. Perhaps Camus is my heart and Aron my head?

Disliking his lack of rigour, I think, again, is more a stylistic preference than anything else. And that it is not a true indictment of the finer components of his thought despite the less methodical nature of his words, its contradictions, compared to his contemporaries or to professors who still lack his moral punch.

That while he himself would deny the label of *philosopher*, and never claimed to be a philosophical genius, it is precisely the honesty and modest sentiment of Camus, who knew his subject and his limitations, his doubting self, that gives his own tempered philosophy—his style and his politics—a strength over that which was extant to him in his reaction to tyrannies, and what, with prescience, he said would likely come after him. In his farsightedness, he saw how easy it was to desecrate the present: with futurisms that would exhort the need for violence and a disregard of its consequences for better tomorrows, or presents—skybound or earthly—and likely not of any reality. Aron would agree but in a more thorough, cooler sociological dimension that would give his literary flair more credibility.

The flat condemnation of a particular ability does not remove some truth, and designating the man as more literary than philosophical points to an implicit contradiction (being *meaningful* while describing meaninglessness) that Camus astutely recognised, and chose to live with regardless in order to live better. *Lettres à un ami allemand* easily and straightforwardly shows this love of our insisted meaning within the obvious thought of a meaningless nothing. Need I cover this man with an extended biography? He fits my own description. He was weary. He could not give everything an explanation. He could not order all of the world under definitions, such as a *philosopher* would attempt to. Again, to think philosophically and without contradiction is to think in a facile way. Even though his thought may be less studious and painstaking, the actual point of the man was nobler—a truer response to anomie than death. One may not wish to follow his line of argumentation, or note the ironies, yet it is difficult to come away from reading him and not feel that one's own vision has been remedied.

Hannah Arendt declared him 'the best man in France' and was likely very right in doing so. He offers more that merits praise and more to live kindly by, as a reluctant

moralist—perhaps one of the best *moralistes* of his time
or since—than those equally, creatively, but wrongly and
irresponsibly *engaged* in his contemporary debates—or otherwise disposed to harmful readings and defiantly harmful
practices. His anxieties still mean a lot; if anything more
so than the concerns of those who succeeded him. We still
have *guillotines* to get rid of and we still have murder to
contend with. Suicide is still as important as Camus' apho-
ristic opening in *Le Mythe de Sisyphe* suggested it was; even
in its simplest form notwithstanding any change in formal
tendencies or in the cultural landscape. I can only recommend more thorough readings of and on figures so easily
misconstrued. Fame colours the perception we have of dead
men and women . . . let alone those still living. Yet it doesn't
take much reading to move beyond misunderstanding. And
Camus isn't too difficult. There are those given false definition to make it easier to bring them down. . . The *sentiment* was always more important than the pernickety stuff,
in the end. Ultimately what is the case? What use was *rigour*
if it did not need to overcome an emotion? It certainly has
its place but that cannot come with the substitution of better conduct—where one is meticulous but for awful reasons.
What use is exactitude if you cannot overcome arrogance
and murder? I do not suggest throwing all scholastic rules
to the wind, which would be the easy and stupid inference—
to think that is what's being advocated would be insulting.
Tony Judt would say that we need a basic chronological understanding of history and context before we set about in-
terrogating the story. We need a basic order of data before
thinking of the past under a narrow lens as a set of prejudices
and lies, i.e. moralising history before understanding it. To
avoid misunderstanding I want to make a brief distinction
between lazy historiographies that take a moralising stance
before prudent understanding of time and place and those

others who believe they are doing correct and precise philosophical and historical work because they are conforming to particular rules or frameworks and established traditions that have more of a political bent than one of historical honesty.

And these are easy substitutes for intellectual responsibility. Moral and/or political judgements need to be made not merely for a world rigorously described, but better understood. What I mean by *sentiment* is that if you are to extract a moral story from a philosophical treatise or a study of history (or to be a moralist in the vein of someone like Camus, who was not the best academic), your predilection towards those ends cannot be either lazy moral interrogation or a love of academic formality. What is typical in such exacting standards, which are intelligent and well-written, but not intellectually honest, is bad history. Artsy anarchistic sorts lacking in rigour can be just as annoying as those who care more about grammar than they do action. I simply advocate for better priorities and artistic merits.

As for Camus, in the last analysis . . . Camus was a star, and the forefront literary contribution to my life.

But of my own future . . . the title of this section. What I would write? What can I do? Could I do the above and have *a substantive project which, if brought to bear, would be a detailed system of argumentation and theory aided by past authorities?* Let us be as frank as possible. I would attempt this were it not for my own brevity. I have to be candid with myself about my ability. It is a misfortune that my personal necessities mean I am a frightful and frenetic mind, and my personality would void any serious or formal attempt at this.

I am also far too lazy. I diagnose something irresolvable, and no amount of effort can overcome my end.

A careful, loathing, dithering experience of illness stymies me. I'm just too ill to write so full a treatise, and I fear that much of this writing is a form of masturbation. My possible ability to get slightly better within the confines of my state is also hard to reach by mental motivation. I can't easily do as others do. Maybe I stray too far into pre-Freudian complexes and fetishise my limitations? I am not sure how I could escape myself anyway. It must be stressed that I am simply unable—lacking mental and physical fortitude. I can recognise and scrutinise this block, but not painlessly and I have to concede the prognosis. My ills, pathology, its restriction and extent, foil my possibilities in study or work, but I cannot resign myself to doing nothing. I have an odd lack of working responsibility which means a bemusing sort of freedom. But that freedom from convention obviously has its own horrors. If I do not have the room to study so deeply then I will make room for art.

Unless some miracle amends what has always been maintained of my upcoming fate, then I can hint at what I had wanted, I can show a glimpse of greater things by association, and perhaps I can show some memorial to what I was for those dearest to me—as a final reprieve for my wearied self.

I will continue a project of love.

CORRESPONDENCE, LOVE

I reject an idea of romanticism, and how it pressures one to forcibly engage in love on pain of shame. But I do not repudiate a need I cannot live without. Bitterness is my only recourse in ignoring it, I cannot disown beauty, and my own self-entitlement spurs me to love what love should be.

I feel a rare pulse in physical interaction, being usually so alone as I have always been accustomed to, whether through the toil of illness or other shortcomings, loneliness. When I recall my previous words on this same subject—my history of sociability—I recognise an indignant youth, maybe anachronistic, but who is not now alien to me. In the absence of long-term lovers or confidants I reflected upon myself publicly—in publications—as a haphazard replacement. I created a novelty in the act of publishing to help myself and my esteem.

I have always thought I can scrutinise my social impotence well, my own representation of my character, my own peculiarity and my own faults and reckoning. I have a history of self-isolation that is easier to describe than explain. The suspicion still lingers that this is my own inefficiency, but I am not a flop or inept once set in most social interactions. I grow vulnerable in boisterous crowds, but in other groups or one-on-one I am mostly eloquent. I face instead a struggle to prioritise correspondence, and its realisations made in hindsight which I am sure are common to many.

I've always attributed a disconnected solipsism to my own interactions, as in with friends, that makes it difficult if I am attempting to manage things, for manifold reasons. I struggle to analyse the finer points of this without destroying my self-worth or being left empty.

I know there is a lot to me that causes this poor performance. Sometimes it is fright, lack of intuition, poor judgement or romantic desperation which creates my trouble with arranging interaction—or I can just as offhandedly ascribe responsibility to sociological events . . . and the alienations of modern communication and messaging. There is another source—being unabashed about announcing my ill-health, once inevitably asked . . . but that can wait.

It is not in the swing of interaction where I am incompetent, or feel useless and inadequate. It is in the preparation, or in retrospection. Reciprocity as and when it happens is not a nervous affair for me. I orate well, I am diligent in listening to those I care for, and I know I care genuinely. Daily ablutions and reflection mean I try to assuage the bitterness that comes from knowing imperfect people; I know with the complexes of pain that impetuousness, rudeness, and anger should not last against minor slights or affronts— so such breakups and forgetfulness I try conscientiously to treat with a necessary forgiveness, often mislaid by many in bouts of annoyance and dejection, as the estrangement from social feeling, this severance, greatly torments the heart and is cruel to all involved.

Wasted time and energy is not something that is contended with easily. In my weaselling attempts I can see things that may be done but I lack the capacity to do them. So what am I aiming for, within myself and my conduct, when I recognise this failure on mine or others' part in social reciprocity? The attempt, so adrift and tantalising, is to make a more prudent use of this suffering and failure without turning to ecclesiastical luggage or false virtue in trying to make sense of them. Suffering has an excellent possible use beyond the sustained, single note of rationalisation that tries to discipline, and then punish, and fool one into the shallows, pretending there is depth. That is to say, I want a better comprehension of social woe when it is extrapolated.

It—lacking bitterness and learning from misdeed—is an effort I see neglected and one I try to maintain with a mature sense, a sort of stoic's responsibility—but a slight is still hard to forget and I have always vainly held the idea that my pathological suffering put me in need of more support—and that was socially neglected.

I could accuse that position of being too indulgent, self-pitying, but rather than condemn, I attempt only to describe it. Others have surely and thankfully attested to my need to be cared for, if I cannot comfortably say so, with my poor sense of self-worth. Being out of loops, the unclearness of reciprocity, antagonisms, things left unsaid; these are hard to wrangle with and I can offer only a mixed and faulty experience. The obscure, heavy hidden lives behind friends you thought you knew, left undeclared, while the course carries on regardless . . .

It is somehow difficult to prepare for being able to do something—logistics—and the difficulty is multiplied by the lack of clarity or the inadequacies common to most communication, and that bothers me. Failed communications in one's various correspondences can still, at least abstractly, be seen for what they are: where embarrassments or acceptable worries cause the breakdown of defined talking, of discerning what your correspondence is and what it means, so they can be more satisfyingly accepted and endured.

We cannot emulate Sartre's idea of social *transparency* in any practical hope, regardless.

The argumentation may not follow, but I begrudge more this ineptitude—an unfitness (mine and others), in the primary organisation of action, events, the prosaic organisation of social life—over the lack of skill or finesse in the act of at least talking, through any means.

Maybe I am fooling myself? That communication recedes and slowly disappears between former friends still causes greater disquiet for me than just failing to see people altogether, and perhaps I simply cannot cope with those failures. I can go long stretches without talking to others, and where technology means easy and instant communication (or the capability of it) there is still the problem of tone and clarity and how these techniques delimit our motivations; how our surroundings change our motivations, e.g. a lack of sincerity as per digital anonymity. The digital world wears a phantom mask that can be seen through, but it is as much eagerly enforced as it is possible to overcome, remove, or use prudently. Perhaps, yet again, I am ruminating needlessly over my own failure to simply organise events? Whatever the case is, I just want more of the vital physicality that I so lack.

I crave the touch I feel is missing in my everyday distress—and I have always felt an absence of conscious care for my social well-being beyond familial and hospitalised attention, if not a lack of awareness in those who do care for me—as I know they do.

But my efforts, we have established, are restricted. I am unable, because of my condition, to further them. I have always felt a lack of social support, but not free to be publicly upset for fear of causing upset, and would always blame myself if I were explicit. I saw intimacy going astray, and the forgotten significance of friendship when abandoned to cliché and neglected as a good subject for discussion. Going out to do something, the scarce chance to discuss Orwell, minor pub visits, a holiday, seem more serious to me when they are flippant things for others. I see friendship and become desperate. There is a physical conditioning of this desperation, though not anything Pavlovian. Illness conditions social view.

I craved, utmost, friends to cry with and save me from what was so tragic—and that could never be retreated from. An unspeakable melancholy. An immovable thorn. When I travel with friends I feel more alive than ever. I simply give in to the common feelings I'd otherwise make distant. Much is said of what it means to travel, and maybe I could add to that later . . .

I am still being indirect, and maybe I should taste my own words and give clearer examples . . .

I am as upfront with my condition as I can be, without being too morose. I'm fine being comedic on my own terms, as I cannot seamlessly live or love with people while lying about my many sufferings and hospital visits and treatments, and it would be impossible to lie about them as well as wrong. This honesty is appreciated by some, if disquieting, but it has always been an obstacle to the possibility of love and romance. This may be my most earnest worry, over friendship, whatever miniature differences there are.

Some stiff and snotty Englishman deals with romantic passions—it seems old hat . . .

Once the reality is exposed there may be few willing to enjoy or accept this masochism. Descriptions of symptoms, the prognosis, things I will be explicit about, some minds can forget them and live in the moment or perchance accept a cold reality . . . but with no miracle cure in sight I am to be left as this expiring, chronic being.

I have been rejected after intimacies through fear, cowardice, worry or a meek concern for doing me harm. You speak of what you are and you could lose everybody. It is somehow, in a mixed and subtle way—speaking to me—like speaking to the recently bereaved: but rather with a slow persistence that won't leave unless you are dishonest, lying, or constantly deflect from what looms in you as you engage just in regular conversation. You are a reminder to happy couples, the blissful, to those with sustainable dreams . . . that it could all crumple and crumble into naught.

To love that man, and the image he promotes? Is it puerile to say that is a form of self-harm?

This accusing of oneself is not to crush others—as judge-penitent. I do not confess my own sins and deprived body to condemn others. My solitude cannot be my pedestal from where I flaunt and punish. I need to be reminded that I am not being vindictive, nor exclamatory, but saddened: descriptive of one's own malady as an honest illustration.

No enterprise with such intense expectations could fail so regularly as love, in any case. But in this case? It is a massive compounding of what is already a harsh trial. I feel a greater sensitivity, time-bound pressure, the heightened temporal exigency, and more a want of honesty. Even with maturity we cannot so easily overcome our disappointment in failed love, and despite the immensity of my pain I manage a dutiful, even forced judiciousness and patience a lot of the time. Do I have the currency for that? There's the trepidation that I don't, and that I would do better to show people their shortcomings, their cavalier disregard, and help them to grow in their integrity and wonderful potential by revealing myself to not be misunderstood: no matter how painful it would be for them to be an example of shattering taboo.

To give them the light of death may be better than leaving them adrift, some may say.

Do I demonstrate care by showing people the dire consequences of their bad actions or allow them the bliss of clemency? I still don't know.

Transparent or not, I create a precedent for the possibilities of future living, of prolonged love, and I outline a need for expedience in my want of lusts as well as more substantial affairs of the heart. I need to live and love quickly before time is spent.

Achieving worldly wisdom in humility and self-awareness still does not prepare one for the final experience, for real grief, through plan or prediction. Virtuous instructions don't prepare us, coolly, for the experience of agony. We cannot inoculate ourselves, or tranquillise ourselves—outside of words—with supreme effectiveness. We're too impotent and the mind isn't the psychic inquisitor of the heart. It's a poor old man giving occasional advice and direction. It may not be followed, and maybe sometimes it shouldn't. I won't say definitely and I lack the intelligence.

Circumstances frame perception and thought at any one time, and it is important to remember that strange but very obvious fluidity.

Of lost love: when another mistake occurs it opens a holistic lens, everything hits me at once, where the specific act of losing someone, whether it is clean and amicable or half-aware and stoned, is seen as an integral part of the sum of illness and my condition. With the loss of that distraction, I am once again opened to seeing naked what I can normally cover up—to what being chronic, and soon enough terminal, means for anything I would do and be.

Looking through these lenses: being in terminal shoes provides some perverse satisfaction—in some respects—by setting the boundaries clearly. One can work to the deadline and explain your death in stern words for people to plan around. Being chronic, from birth disposed to differently look at things, there is a dim purgatory. We can try to trace the clouded lines between mental, chronic, and terminal phenomenology. We can note their intersections, but here the description offered—of both love and life—is the rarer sort of long-worn, hard-learned, life-long suffering under progressive illness that has a neglected literature compared to the frequent suddenness of terminal scares or the erratic life of depressive mentalities. These categories are not wholly distinct, but in some measure need defining if only for my ease.

With this view, there's a rationalisation of feeling in order to cope with it, with the difficulty chronicity brings to love lost, but this comes at some expense where there is a struggle to make room just to feel what I am feeling without shame. I fear my own bitterness, the reproach that is deserved, what another deserves in kind; and you beat yourself up over feeling passionate in your failure. So there's that which needs to pass each time . . . but when you live to love again, there is still the fear of your time being more precious than others, a coerced view of lost time, and the result is often a bleak self-seriousness covered with dry humour, a little frantically, and weary in its conscious dread.

I have always loved in my strained and worried way so many things about others, even those that go beyond what I could ever understand. No matter what misgivings I have or compromises I can see the need for, I cannot change much about those I love without feeling guilty—and in wanting major changes to one's lovers one shows how they fail in loving, and harm those they adore. Nothing is enough for them and they dream with so much ambition. They become most adept at dreaming of new obligations, yet another each day, yearning for what they cannot discover and for fresh new demands. And then there are those who don't deserve love . . . I am left with a knowledge that love can't wait so long. A shared bedroom, a hand held in yours, I can't see much else that matters. It is not puerile or quaint to say it. It is just too commonly said in dull and repetitive ways, emptily, without a real heart to it. What diktats are so urgent and demanding? Do you need these patterns and strategies? I can't fulfil most, if any, and there's the prospect of worse things that take priority: fear, a most awful of things. A fear of being alone before I go.

These are the layers that make loving so much more desperate. The chronic sense is constant, ebbing, the flavour left in your mouth, only sometimes clouded and warped in everyday concerns. You wake dazed at night, soft jazz humming as in some atmospheric cliché, and see the impending menace. You know everybody will face it, but the saying loses its bite and has no real severity. It becomes meaningless to suggest to those full of life that they will meet an end. They will not feel it deep within their bones until too late. I have to stress again, and again, that for those *others*, those I fear hurting (as if one is egregious?) by claiming I'm special . . . their death is far away in their thoughts. We are all in the same boat, as the dull saying goes, with death as the most certain of possibilities.[27] But most could not live, without exhaustion or inertia, in constant fear of random Leviathan attacks that suddenly topple their boat. Their boats are sealed and seaworthy. And if we are to milk the metaphor, they sail in less stormy waters. So they may sail to the many shores they can choose. My boat bears a resemblance, but it's already sinking. Born with the water already lapping at your feet, and what shores can you choose to set sail to? Failure seems more disastrous. What shore where there's a hand to hold can you get to when the water

[27] 'death is the most certain of possibilities'—Martin Heidegger

is at your neck and you barely have a boat left? Drowning is imminent. Maybe I can be permitted this gloomy solipsism? Maybe I am allowed it after denying it so much, through fear of giving offence? Having been assured that it is okay to say things and note these real phenomenological differences, can I have this?

I am allowed my boat metaphor.

No one properly appreciates the cliché of urgency to life because vehicles could hit and kill you; they can live and ignore and be young and free and it is enviable. I am crudely poetic here, rather than attesting to psychological realities to substantiate the claim that death, illness and dying are not often confronted. I have done that before, I guess.

The Denial of Death[28] will hold true, with the *heroic sense of immortality* still vibrant and gripping. Since birth my body was known to fall short, where most would have a far greater chance to thrive and protected from the commonplace alarm at disability. Few conduct themselves on the *'what if'* of remotely possible accidents tomorrow, and less tormented are they by darkness visible. They do not ache so hauntingly and consistently in their everyday moves. They do not live by laboured breaths and can stand still most days without their bodies buckling, and they can run without dying in coughs and rasps. And when they do cough they do not feel the ripple of quakes and aftershocks course through their body as a forceful reminder of a protracted bodily reality.

They are not slowly dying by chronic measure, they live with an attitude and manner of life unto life and not unto death, and their own pain is something else; by any reckoning a little less terrible, less persistent, and a little easier to endure through their happy distractions. It is not dismissive of them to say that. You hear it from them. They've said it

---

[28] *The Denial of Death* (1973) by Ernest Becker.

to me as they offer false hope and plan things for 20 years time. They don't speak death's name and disbelieve the disabled's case. There are, too, the ubiquitous sorts that spit at wheelchairs and those with leprosy—they dismiss entire lives. Life itself, even.

There are those far worse off than I am. What of it? There is no real solace in the abstract measure of 'at least I'm not as bad as that'. You cannot minimise your pain that way unless you enjoy a vulgar sadism. Do not lie about your pain, Jake. The subsisting ill are still a minority. Some afflictions are brief, act towards the fact of death quickly, and not so sustained and drawn out.

I'll be told of such energetic lives, be witness to them, and remain out of their reach. I cannot *'get action'* (cf. Theodore Roosevelt).[29] The myriad problems we all face to our differing degrees will seem just as severe to each of us, but different conditions mean different horizons and different ways of life. My own draws me hastily in to confront mortality, whether I was presupposed to existential query or not. When you know so young that your life is destined to an early fate, that is much more pressing than fortune's possibility of being in some chance accident sometime next week. You know you would go, you feel different, you live in another world, and you have less time for nonsense. But difference and the closing distance also enables you to ask questions—about yourself and also about others. To live exhaustively on abstract death, not just on definitive death . . .

'To gather ye rose buds' is usually, despite film trope, a bravery out of range: off the array.

Infirm and ill: many may still not face the bare truth, and may conclude in naïve belief to avoid it. . . but with me, I

---

[29] Quote from Theodore Roosevelt. 'Get action. Do things; be sane; don't fritter away your time; create, act, take a place wherever you are and be somebody.'

think warily and am conscious of being haughty, I am *forced
to nausea* and feeling—unable to trick myself and so simply
dispel it. Morbidity imposes itself as a watchful guardian.
On my shoulder my companion sits unresting. To not see
death as an intrinsic part and not act with it, despite its obvi-
ousness, is not just an ignorance of everyday occurrence. It
is not keeping in the front of one's mind . . . the dirty facts of
war: what not seeing death produces in thought and action.
The attitude relies on an obliviousness that would falter if
it saw, truthfully, Oblivion. We revel in high concepts over
what is small and real, and cheapen life itself.

> To answer your own question: Why did all of this
> happen to me? You gaze at everything with a parting
> and slightly sorrowful look . . . Almost from the other
> side . . . No longer any need to deceive anyone or your-
> self. It's already clear to you that without the thought
> of death it is impossible to make out anything in a hu-
> man being. Its mystery hangs over everything. War is
> an all too intimate experience. And as boundless as
> human life . . .
>
> —Svetlana Alexievich, *The Unwomanly Face of War*

Most will not recognise, beyond brief moments, life
with illness as its primary theme. . . a sort-of Heideggerean
living, every day, under the purview of death and threaten-
ing, life-shortening illness. Ideology will always favour a tomorrow, politics will look forward to what is out of sight . . .
but in the long run we're all dead. Montaigne wished to dis-
sipate death by facing it head-on. This meant keeping it *in
mind*. A trying task really . . . most noble effort. What sure
and gentle guidance that man gave on facing death.

A majority will live as if they might not die at all, making use of their present time, no matter what death sur-
rounds them in the undertaker's office or at the nurse's sta-

tion. It is the guy next to you in the trench that dies. Not you. It couldn't be you . . .

This is certainly no condemnation of nurses, to whom I owe my life. They do hard and necessary work, and it would be imprudent to suggest that death is an entirely forgotten quantity when many people may live more nobly in the light of death than I can see. But the tangled psychology of death and its mental distancing—the usual way we live and forget—persists.

Experiencing one's life with a view to mortality, especially one's own mortality, and without the daily interruptions of lively business and activity, is made more likely through a direct self-experience of feeling tangibly weak, dying, delicate, debased and shortened in one's own breaths; or a closeness to these things through work as a daily reminder. That does not mean the ill are virtuous by that case and are revealed to truth, but the confrontation of bodily fact and the reaching of conclusions on the use or uselessness of actions can be achieved more easily—rightly or wrongly. You are closer, for obvious reasons, to the realities of death and its implications—and pressured more than others to see it and *think*.

Do I want to force the reality of death? The premise? Slam my fist on the desk and shout at them to look at it? I want to force that humility. Even if the victim is left only in conflict, stuck on the fault line, remaining disorganised would be better than living so confidently while *not dying and living forever*. It is hard to press home the fact. Inner turmoil becomes incommunicable apart from those fleeting moments when understanding becomes clearer—under pressing circumstances. And often, exposing to the ignorant their own offensiveness in not seeing the ill—either humiliating them or kindly awakening the realisation in them—can be upsetting not just to them but to me too.

It is hard to be in the best mood and speak about illness politely all the time, to be well-behaved in pain, and live sweetly for others' sake.

Once, at university, I was alone in my room, reading or likely doing nothing. Tired as usual, unable to take out and organise my medications so it would be easier to administer them and my treatments later. Independence is difficult enough when one is healthy. When unhealthy . . . well, it's obvious. I was sat alone and wanted to move. Fatigue and lethargy always take over and time would be spent asleep, not doing anything, spiralling down as I failed to care for myself. So I forced myself out to walk. I needed supplies and something to drink, so collected myself and went out. At first walking is fine, then one forgets oneself and walks too far. I would struggle walking back home. I over-estimated myself, desperately trying to exercise and be healthier, but did not want to go home empty-handed. Nor could I retrieve a proper shopping inventory. I wouldn't be able to carry anything beyond a small bag with some snacks as anything more, fine for others, would be too heavy for me. Even then my extra light bag felt too heavy, and upon exiting Sainsbury's my body suffered. I cannot often acclimate to temperature changes without violent coughing, shaking, and feeling stiff. I was already disheartened and it was gruelling enough, when a member of the public decided to comment.

Explicitly visible disabilities come with their own challenges when it comes to accessing support—lower visibility adds another dimension. Sometimes comments are offhand, or said jovially. I thankfully haven't suffered the most disgusting of offences where the ill are not believed or belittled and publicly emasculated by those with no understanding.

But this nasal, shrill, and baffled old woman decided to poke, with a biting tone, at the fact that I was coughing horribly and in some pain, rather than offer help or aid. Why?

Why take time out of her day to say anything? Why are people so preoccupied? Why this happy sadism? Normally, I would just humiliate the person bluntly. 'No. I have a disease and will be dead very soon.' Most do not comment further after that. This would go against my thought to not *flaunt* myself and my case, and I live with these regrets. But with this person, I had a weight upon me and I decided to destroy them. Not only did I declare my death—I declared hers.

I wished for it. I called her every name under the sun as if this 'bloodless cunt' with zero understanding somehow deserved Hell for being so utterly stupid, inane, and crude in her remarks. In that moment she represented all people who knew nothing of psychology, or death, or of the entire gross human condition.

I felt awful after that. I did not need to insult this stranger. Teary and further disheartened, I left her blank and upset and commenced the long, long walk home. I couldn't call anyone to come and fetch me, and I would have to very literally drag my ailing body back to my bed. I fell straight asleep. Who benefitted from any of that?

One can be anaesthetised to events by their regular proximity. By the metronome tick. The frequency itself can armour us against infirmity and facilitate our basic functions and processes—to live more easily. Disorder, panic, and trauma are par for the course when *esprit de corps* and your unconscious guard are worn down by the violence of shitting yourself, lungs collapsing, and forgetting your parents exist or losing childhood memories every day. I want to believe that it is possible for people to see the defining cessation that is death, because I want at least the slim positivity of seeing that. I want care, from that. In nearly any faith, culture, class or upbringing, it is possible to encounter the dying and learn what it is to die through the only view we can have. We are mortal: that may be, and the heaven posed by those offering grand absolution, *the fix*, is yet again empty. There might be a next life, but how little comfort that is when facing the lime-pit, the executioner's pistol . . . and I cannot bother with it anyway. If I try to, I only feel that I am deceiving myself. If our lot is complete annihilation then at least let us live justly; and not have our impending Oblivion seem as if *it* were justice. Death and illness and what these represent can be countenanced. Surely they can be learned from? Surely we can show love to what dies? An intuitive understanding of infirmity and deprecation comes from being ill—is at least possible from there—from unrecoverable illness, in a way more immediately apparent than if one can live more freely and healthily. There is a gulf between cultures: the Dying and the Immortal. Death is a thing, the most definite thing. It is as inescapable as anything else except by the most risky and fraudulent of leaps.

> The remedy the vulgar use is to not think on it; but from what brutish stupidity can they derive so gross a blindness?

—Michel de Montaigne

No matter the basic truths; the unconscious pervasiveness of immortality, through whatever biological or psychological condition, will forever hold such sway that humility will be more difficult than hubris. It is a vile world, and one can forget that. I see a need instead to face it. I need to find my solace in that.

My body and mind are aged before their time. I react instinctively to youth and have the response of a jaded old man; it is an unfortunate test of my patience. I stare blankly, but my remorse is neither defined nor refined. I will fail at doing good. I will fail at telling those I love the things I should tell them, and finally, after all the talk, I will still feel an emptiness. My time is more costly, and I feel that with a gripping severity. But to act? Improbable. That would require energy. To not be a sloth. To remove this barrier, burn it, destroy it: no. It is a special fear, a unique way of being scared; I don't have the currency to live unfearing and my terror is an exceptional terror beyond the others that walk straight in the street. Am I too derisive? I really, really do fear that. The fury of realisation wears me out, a savage reminding, draining my colour and making me a pallid thing. The phenomenology of illness sets a tone, the sordid detail becomes too bare and, again, a clinging morbidity remains. There is something similar to what anyone would experience, but compounded, enforced, and given a new sheen. Being brave does not give a true reprieve—one is not let free, and the horror of death is not resolutely assuaged by any easy measure from being either stern or otherwise scared. But it must be seen. And through that—the isolating gnaw of impending doom, others can still carry on, unremembering. I feel deeply selfish, alone, but there's little you can do to amend the position you're placed in, gifted an inquisitorial gaze; even with styled words a permanent vacation from grave thoughts is inaccessible.

So this is my case. And, in part, what love is in my case. How on earth am I to get over this? Should I? I clinically note the boundaries of romanticism, I clinically note my health, but I cannot crush my feelings through a process of equal pain and forgetfulness. I should not be dishonest. I may not be alone, but I will, primally, feel alone and unconnected: helped to *overcome* neither by others, nor by philosophy— beyond the appealing concord of propaganda from those decent, open-minded and open-hearted beings that I can feel some affinity with. Affinity, but not a full reconciliation of grief, is all I can hope to maintain. Philosophy won't reason out our anguish, but simply being exposed may reveal something true—an instinctual sympathy that may grant me a small measure of contentedness.

I am given the ability to expound on grief by my proximity. I cannot permit myself an ignorance in some form of bliss from what is upsetting. This moroseness has formed me, I can see that, and I can choose to weakly hide it or show its true colour. I don't want a dark literature—I need what is redemptive, but not what is a lie.

Looking at this writing in a disassociated way, it reflects something I see sometimes as admirable, and is most admirable when I see what is written as sage advice from another. But there is always the difference between recognition and actually being capable of the endeavour. When I see others having to deal with recent deaths I am often speechless, as I think that saying something for the sake of it is empty at best and insulting at worst. Funeral platitudes tire me. They even offend me. Those ceremonies, so acted and choreographed, the insular superficiality of rituals . . . they seem to terrify us more than the fact of death itself, or otherwise exacerbate the pain of mourning by persuading the unthinking to make a spectacle for a day, only to return to their daily apathy thereafter. The very notion of one's *deathbed*, surrounded by deathly dressed figures in deathly silence, not even speaking of the word 'death' as if they'd utter the name of the Devil himself? One may as well be dead already.

They set artefacts about to fawn over and weep, they act upon death as if attending a rare function, nor would they really give the arational detail of death its full face as they turn to platitudes. Death can be more palatable when we are spared having to prepare grand ceremonies. A brusque state-ment, but I haven't had many good funeral experiences . . .

For most ceremonies that is. A few can create good cele-brations, but others, most others, have restricted reflections made more morose than they ought to be. But we aren't all in New Orleans. And ultimately, the agony is not con-tended. It is let out in the brief spectacle—and the *everyday* continues. The strangeness of death is not disarmed. A fa-miliarity is lacking—amidst one's jolly steps and road jour-neys, death is an infrequent thought. Where it is frequent for some, it is oppressive rather than liberating. Few are truly worth listening to on this immense question. The diarist Barbellion is one of the best. The task or effort I would have in mind is to see the fact of dissolution as a liberating thing, while not being possessed by it, or creating a fetish. Death in fancy dress doesn't help me.

A certain temperament is needed, ultimately, where to consider our inescapable death means to give what *is* . . . its vitality. For enough of us, nothing is faced in the end. To live, to learn to live, to *philosophise* as if to learn to die . . . how rare a thing that is.

When I see others dealing with their own questions, I can offer something but my words might be empty no matter my intention. I touch on something unhappy, no happy death, and again I get, as I am told, to set a tone. It feels selfish to speak about *all of this*. I feel undeserving of love, and have a ruined sense of self-esteem. Yet if I am able to make the pain of some others less terrible by my own example, then I feel I should give a hand to those I care for. I'm not for public duty, but I want a voice that can't be seen to be so vain. If I cannot do anything else, I want to care for those dear to me. And so I leave them my sentiments.

I can fault myself for all my woe despite outside assurances—and I have had to be told to remove my hate for myself, and to be made to listen—that even though I am in a desperate situation, even though I might need more love and care than most, that does not mean people get to trample my precious heart outstretched and beating in my hand.

THE END OF CHRONICITY

As I continue to grapple with when my demise will be, and the uneasy course of those last few years that are up for grabs, it is natural that I grow a little more depressive no matter what lofty set of approximate ideals I invoke.

I see the idealised standard of the stoic which we seem to want to preach. I'm rather dubious about it—not a complete rejection, but a desire to temper it. This is an undercurrent analogous to the downward trend of my bodily health: receding, gruelling, with fluctuations but an inevitable decline that foresees no repair. With what impression I can give of myself and my feeling, it is a conflict that is not exclusively between principle and natural emotion that governs me. These terms, again, are not mutually exclusive and will intersect. I aspire to loving affirmations in the face of a darkness. They are held in the adored words of others who I admire, their lives, and the possibilities still available regardless of fate. They mix with a guttural sadness, a tragicomedy, an upset at the world but more an awful distress at myself and my perceived inability.

Every day I wake and have to wash myself of a deep melancholy that flows beneath any easy talk. If it isn't melancholy, there are days where I am simply numb, as if I were a gormless animal who doesn't know where it is. I can stare, as a cat might, at a wall for aimless hours—thinking of nothing (though it would be nice to think a cat thus occupied is musing happily).

Under all my pretence, there is a child that shrieks and doesn't want any of this evil, any pain, the dread of being dead, and I would soon, and with a worrying haste, end it all. Treatments are painful. Stop that. Medicating. Stop that. Exercises and long car journeys. Etc. etc. etc. . . . Please stop.

The process of thinking upon this becomes a tragic, then comic thing; I must confusedly mitigate what is so dire and dreadful within me. Whether that be through some form of humour (one that makes some light of our absurdity—à la Beckett), or—if not that—then an unabashed frankness. I'm concerned that I'm too depressive, that the view from the likes of Groucho Marx, or *Beyond the Fringe*, etc.—making light of the thought that nobody knows what they're doing or what's going on—would be better than the similar themes coming morosely and more frighteningly from a Franz Kafka. But I'm afraid I lack that capacity for wit. I guess I like to be funny, but I don't think I can be *that* funny. To countenance this particular weariness every day is foreign to those I'd describe it to, and is the hardest feeling to convey.

I regularly have to go through courses of IV antibiotics and other medications (the details become less important) . . . The regularity of these procedures hurts me—it is a slow reminder of what afflicts me and what will come. Heavier interventions—surgeries, great risks, and the possibility of utter failure—are all calculated in both icy and sentimental ways. Parental wishes, medical demands, they are all weighed and judged in the kaleidoscopic mess of conflicting reason and emotion.

I am not here to pander to those medical specifics, rightly or wrongly, as I would not want to bore with formal details or hospital notes. The hardest thing to convey of my understanding is what I am faced with at the remote prospect of *getting better*, when I am shown the successes of others, and the chance of a slightly healthier living. This is always abstracted. The complexes of another are seen as if they could fit seamlessly upon your own delicate situation, where force of motivation and action will surely help and straighten out the whole mess.

A whole life of experiences goes into developing what one is; the thought of histories abstracted, people abstracted, ideas taken as tokens applicable to anything with enough finesse or with brute force—I have never been able to accept this. It is equal parts anachronism, obtuse solipsism, a taking of one's own boundaries as those of the world and anyone else. To flatly reject those assumptions seems scary. To be frightened and terrified at 'returning' to a possible normalcy you never had: how can they not see that? There is the faintest chance of a new life I cannot invest hope in.

So much optimistic weight is put into the hope of fascinating technologies and new developments. For some it seems easier to invest in them, with or without illness. But again we must note the difference of ill experience. To raise yourself up so high in that hope only to crash in inevitable failure you've been preparing for, many years in the making, with so many peers already gone; it needs to be seen how such experiences wear and bear down on you.

It is passionately wished that faced with bright new circumstances I should react with ease, as a matter of protocol, and that my entire mismanaged mess of thought and experience would mean I am not set to fail—fulfilling my own prophecy, or not.

No matter if events could somehow, by their miracle, refute me . . . someone will have this anchor. Death still comes, and new transhuman developments are pitiable, as of yet. And even with their becoming there is the elementary philosophical mess. The drive to make it all better is so desperate that it can lead to nightmare denouements.

Stressed out, everyday shit, makes it hard to foster a solidarity of feeling for more than a passing moment. Demands will supersede immodest and impractical terrors. My grief is not so animated and active always, but numbing and immobilising. This doesn't reflect the usual picture of what despair is considered to be. It is the *wrong* mode of grief—as we seem to have more sympathy for outbursts and shock than with what creeps up on you slowly and looms—that speaks in desperate whispers and walks with crooked steps.

One is expected to be contented and positive, yet any apparently real and lasting happiness would always arouse the suspicion that something is wrong, and melancholy will still face gross reproach. In seeing what is saddening, culture is disgusting. It is insulting. It lacks a true engagement with or consistent awareness of frailty. I cannot begin to fathom the chemical mix of interventions in my health, throughout my whole life; and the resultant psychology produced is a sore imposition. I may not espouse some ratomorphic behaviourism, but life's stricter influences should be noted.

'All of what I do in *philosophy* is bundled with the refuse of illness.'[30]

There's damage done, and I have to find another course of endurance.

My *philosophy* has to be an alleviation of immediate and prolonged pain, simply to allow me to subsist, let alone live. It is not a curiosity first found in any derivative Aristotelean 'wonder', so inert, which eventually sucks you in to its own steel trap. Thinking you may out-think things. Epistemology *proper*: alone? No. I see traps in the first step. And I need to actually help myself.

---

[30] Quoting myself.

How to make use of physical pain, more so prolonged disease: when the whole heart, mind, spirit—these are synonymously used terms and I austerely side with the boring accounts of what a person's essential element is—when one's whole emotion turns inwards and petrifies, if it cannot openly weep: this is an understated awfulness. Poetry can attempt to reflect the substance of this, to communicate the idea, but it often falters at expressing the calamity. Does poetry really paint the war well? It is rare for it to do so. One could wholly reject the limits of everything, embrace what lies beyond the possibility of real scrutiny —a type of intellective suicide that is beyond my reach. Or you could more prudently accept the starkness of the tragicomedy. Naked to the unknown. Facing it. Always facing it—the baffled indecision. It is humbling that my burdensome tones might not merely be annoyances; that I could give a touching assurance and fraternity by saying something, and not hiding my woes. I have comrades under siege by the same malady; I can give them the friendship of a shared experience. The sublime service of a language of the dying—to squeeze the hand of these intimate peers so bereft of their warmth. To speak into the ether and be received.

I wrote earlier of being unable to build oneself with just oneself. It was more obvious why when I felt so alone. When you fear the bitterness of solitude, and how painful and frightening it would be. To maintain themselves, most would need the Hell of others. To revel in pure solitude is unavailable to me.

A point needs to be made and repeated as it never seems to find purchase. Considering cases of individual pain *worse* or *better* than my own—applying this apparently quantitative measure—does not help me. That is why I can feel inconsiderate, and reticent, about saying I am different to most, that I am rarer; as their own suffering, by my confession, would seem meagre and devalued—or so they might think. To say all other sufferings under the most abject are not worth concern by that reference is a destitute lie, a sub-terfuge and deflection, and it does not make one's own death any easier that it comes later.

Children suffering in distant lands don't make one's worries worthless, nor do those atrocities constitute a monopoly on suffering. Instead, what I can do is foster a natural liking and comprehending of something—and a guidance I cannot myself easily conform with. In suffering we cannot afford to be competitive.

Disability and illness, and what they represent in all their variances, have an existential weight attached to them. They are then often deliberately overlooked, undervalued, with their representations preferred dead or out of the way. One of the most fundamental aspects of existence is viewed instead as a narrow lens, a niche, rendered as unimportant or as malignant—out of fear, shame, utilitarian malevolence or stock ignorance. Misunderstood and put at a distance. Dis-ability and its implications are reviled as they're not a com-fortable presence for many people.

Popular culture in any nation will not contend with pain, grief, illness, or disability (not always synonymous, but still) in any truly commendable or genuine way. We simply do not cope with life. Disability or ill-health is viewed as a per-sonal failure to not work or do better before it is compre-hended simply as reality—often inescapable reality. And the needs of disabled people will always come after the needs of those who aren't so when it most matters. Casual eugen-ics is the preferred state of affairs for many of us before accepting disabled life. Whole industries, much of civilisation, even, is dependent on making illness an easily comprehensible personal fault and truly escapable through enough effort, money, or spirit. Values held so commonly deem life worthless if it cannot be 'productive' in what is ultimately a terrible way to spend our short time.

Heaven forbid you make the *healthies* uncomfortable. One better not present a less than heroic image, lacking any glitzy optimism, no hard grit, or show anything that may make them a little upset. If illness is not presented in a way that makes those who aren't ill or disabled comfortable, in their aloof world removed from real concerns, then good luck. Allow me to be a bit miserable. Or if I am somehow jovial, I don't need false hope.

Pain and its minimisation, being able to be merely comfortable with the tiniest reprieve, is more important to me than most else. I am too ambivalent towards continuing life if doing so means being in an amount of pain than makes prolonging not worth the cost. This doesn't then mean drugging me into complete catatonia so I feel nothing. I simply want to live without being so exhausted, without so much stress, before my premature death that I am absolutely terrified of. I don't want to shorten my life, but I end up being complacent and unable to do things that would prolong it because they cause too much discomfort and distress.

The callous then suggest that not being able to stoically handle such pain is weakness or a moral failing. I will reserve using the worst words that I have for them.

I repeat that these people live in an entirely different and dismissive universe unattended to some of the most vital rudiments of the human condition—which involve sickness and disability. They believe the conceit that rendering life through the lens of disability is reductive, rather than experiencing life with a more essential primary theme. Obviously this does not mean that sick or disabled people are now soothsayers or immediately more knowing of the truth, and I hold no room at all for fetishisation or self-flagellating glorification, but, rather . . .

> . . .this matter of ill-health is more personal, more es-
> sentially of the ego than anything in the world; more
> than love, for that can be given expression; more than
> religion, because that is a satisfaction in itself; more
> than fear, for that passes. Pain is personal, before ev-
> erything. Only one who has experienced it in some
> measure can understand its significance in life.
>
> —Richmond H. Hellyar in *W. N. P. Barbellion* (1926)

I just want some respite, even if true peace is impossible. Just treat people a little better.

In this untidy mix comes a taut balancing. Austerity with unfetteredness, acceptance with revolt, sceptical one day and the next day an Epicurean.

This is a continued use of high concepts ham-fistedly describing basic understandings, and here it does a sad job in defining things improperly, unreasonably, rejecting and affirming itself equally. I value the wisdom of others immensely, who could with an enviable strength marvel at life and want to live enduringly. And if I could, I would just follow those words. They have words that go beyond anything I could say. I've said them to myself and understood them from those I admire, but I am still my own problem. Seeing something sage is fine in recognition, but I'm still emotional, worn, and tired. I can write down an ideal but whether I can conform to it or not is out of my control. Ideals are bigger than I am. I have, too, a history of descriptions against life, almost avowing a different sort of early death; but I at least murkily stress their merit as descriptions of passing thought that I see as important to confront. To reject or affirm, again I am always torn.

I can agree with a distaste for the shadowy pseudo-intellectualisation of and by the artistic, but I sit in the artist's seat. To serve, to act justly with the fright of the *Pensées*:[31] I want to be quiet—slow—in the way of being temperate in my inner conduct. In trying a little tenderness. I can have little rush for plans no matter my expedient body. I have to become less tense and reconcile with a defiance while knowing my place. It is a capitulation to inability, though not resigned from life and ideas, served with aware-ness and love.

We return to the beginning of this work . . . the *Strug-gle* . . . I show that I want something fundamental from what is base, what is palpable, what I may taste and squeeze, because I cannot find anything fundamental elsewhere. If I accept a void it is metaphysical, not human. I have to remain sentimental ultimately despite my own coldness. These replayed feelings and tangible sensation hold for me something dear—in the vacancy of the spiritual world. I feel an attachment to this harsh idea of life's general character (what is amoral is still cruel to human emotion); and my self-seriousness, soppy and stern, draws on the repeated point held paradoxically.

Escapism in grandiose terms I find hard to agree with. There is escape in both the vertical aims of faith and the horizontal aims of the secular religions and their own night-mares. I leave no room for dreams, but daily keep taut and revising, as a vital thread, in the treading of the narrow path towards a truthful solidarity. Towards an honesty in our lim-itations before we go about touching wildest fantasies and visions. I can agree to a mild, tamer leisure as a fairer thing. I want to offer solace as I feel so much sorrow, but get stuck in my own worrywart misery. I still want passion with this leisure. I am not overly complacent, there is the fury of lost

[31] *Pensées* (1670) by Blaise Pascal

time; maybe it is *pagan*, meaning heretical? *Greek*. Maybe it would have been nice to be initiated at Delphi? Dionysus speaks necessarily. So does Sisyphus. Remember to scorn Icarus.

A basic idea of physicality is important ... What we cannot see is still terrifying. Fictions created to pretend we don't die won't help me, and nor will false hope in hotel rooms. Physicality is not merely some pale diversion. Hume's backgammon hedonism[32] gives us a proper accord with what we can truly know. The apprehending of what we are confounded by has to be soothed by acknowledgment of the unanswerable, but we should not corrupt our resultant playtime into something that makes us hungry and cold. Into tactless hedonism. A sensualism that is unlimited and utterly naked becomes weak and obtuse. My struggle to hold the physical as paramount is stifled by what I've already said of its misuses; but all maxims will be misheard and misused by some, and we cannot allow them to steal what is dear.

Meaning becomes a skewer to these misusers and misers who would divest and kill us. It is from a comprehension of rudimentary materiality that real flavour comes, rather

---

[32] 'Where am I, or what? From what causes do I derive my existence, and to what condition shall I return? ... I am confounded with all these questions, and begin to fancy myself in the most deplorable condition imaginable, environed with the deepest darkness, and utterly deprived of the use of every member and faculty. Most fortunately it happens, that since Reason is incapable of dispelling these clouds, Nature herself suffices to that purpose, and cures me of this philosophical melancholy and delirium, either by relaxing this bent of mind, or by some avocation, and lively impression of my senses, which obliterate all these chimeras. I dine, I play a game of backgammon, I converse, and am merry with my friends. And when, after three or four hours' amusement, I would return to these speculations, they appear so cold, and strained, and ridiculous, that I cannot find in my heart to enter into them any farther.'—David Hume, *An Enquiry Concerning Human Understanding* (1748)

than models and schemes. Mundane things become more important.

Yet in its replacement of a cosmology of escape my basic physicality cannot become as brutal—urging me horizontally to cruel ends instead of vertically—in a wrongheaded retention of the same hubris. Humanisms of progress amount to the same flaws of spirit without a quiet tempering, a mediation, and sensualism is still our vital aspect, if, *neither weak nor obtuse.*

I must value love, friendship and humour seriously. These common ideals are given such a facile, paltry, scant and ineffectual treatment by so many commentators. The offence these outlets cause is exacerbated when we see that they are taking essential aspects of life only to (again) miser them and turn them into tat to be sold—appealing to our lowest instincts.

Being alone is tough, and requires a strength beyond the ordinary. This is rarely understood and usually expressed with bitter pride. I am not strong. Most are not. We have to be there for each other . . . together in our individual loneliness. Cliché should be seen through and suffering does not become a virtue that solves itself. It doesn't do that. If you keep what is yourself, and are not tranquillised by it, then it will stay. It is a question of coping, not of elimination— what is ill returns and remains.

Dying young is maybe different from dying old, where one could finally be *glad* to end a long toil . . . I am still wary of blunt stoicism. It seems as if it is a sort of subterfuge. A trick. It seems, even, in its cases of public house stupor where ragged men proclaim they should be shot before dementia, as if it would be plain ignorance; and the wish to be shot before hardships is rarely fulfilled. And so many would die . . . naïve? I would be fooled to think elimination of emotion, or the hijacking of positive emotion, was possible and that I could cure the pestilence. I cannot forget wholly, but am allowed to for some time: to function. I cannot make wallowing in the swamp a virtue, and we surely deserve some contentment. It is too hard to be so dreary. I can't be a masochist.

I have escapes, but they can never be absolute. I have unfortunate sights forced upon me, but I cannot be atrophied or left to the wild. They are specious and muddleheaded rationales that suggest we can truly escape the unhappiness and foreboding; that, somehow, what is terrible is easy to endure. To not fear what we cannot feel?[33] We fear *precisely* that we have no more feeling, no more thought, the waste of efforts that cannot be replayed with no eternities to stray into.

To not love, link, nor think; to be annihilated against an essential eking for sustenance. There's the animal fear the dissonant mind could, *could*, weasel itself out of. The body less so. It takes a unique constitution, armoured against its own essence, to find a peace that is not taut and unsure. Or it takes some long-worn and aged wretchedness. Fear cannot be escaped if one wishes to remain alive. Most talk of peace is stasis, and a lie.

To out-reason this heft is to ossify.

I kept something Kantian with me, beside my weary reservations, some duty; I cannot aspire to heroism—to making a virtue of misery (I have never intended to make my de-

---

[33] Reference to Epicurean doctrines. The Tetrapharmakos (τετραφάρμακος) 'four-part remedy' is a summary of the first four of the Κύριαι Δόξαι (*Kuriai Doxai*, the forty Epicurean *Principal Doctrines* given by Diogenes Laërtius in his *Life of Epicurus*).

scriptions, knowing death, *virtuous*)—and I have never had
time for sainthood either—making virtue miserable. I can
only suggest a wisdom in our description of things.

Transcendence does not mean to find mystified eleva-
tion; nor am I to be annulled in the atrophied sensibility of
the ardent rationalist. I never learned to accept myself, and
my narrowed vision, and I really simply should have. Too
much was beyond me and my understanding, all I should
have done was accept.

The *trembling* philosopher, as Voltaire puts it, is desperate to know the world almost fully. So they, the great
framers of definition, if they're archetypal sorts of philosopher, attempt to systematically and as a wholesale ordeal
understand the world as if it had a discernible formulation
for all of its attending parts. When we are simply too feeble
for that. We can touch on things, be thorough taxonomists
in some cases, but it is a matter of aesthetic that says the
world is wholly cogent in our possible perceptions or that
the world is externally made true.

Others can forget these comprehensive projects em-
ployed to comprehend things and live, some tremble in
their subject, and some are naïve enough to think they can
know it all.

In the areas we can examine, in language, in conscience,
what we are, ultimately, to do but give ourselves some le-
nience, and even give up on *knowing it all*, give up reconciliation, or ideal, for our own good and prosperity. There
are still enough things we have a duty to revolt against and
pretexts to say *no* to while recognising the failure of zealous ambitions. It is perhaps a wise move, of a better temper,
to not feel bad about what is beyond you. But it is still difficult. Pride and relief are still possible, while reconciling
the world is not. Summer exists within you without removing the death from winter, and the fragile blossom on the

spindly tree persists. The recurring words within my constraints of vision are not recipes for optimism. We have little
use for those recipes in the extremes of our distress. We long
for rarer words of wisdom and of courage—not absconding
the world or oneself. A vulnerable meaning, frail but defiant,
comes from knowing it all stops. It is not a sad philosophy
one has if they dislike comfortable optimism. The sun and
beauty are still there. What one has: it is sensitive to the
world. *Concerned*, if grave.

It is not soft and merry with escape, nor hardened in ar-
mouring itself against cruelty with cold rationale. It finds
a peace that isn't stasis, which is tautly balanced, equivo-
cal, conflicted and unsettled. We touch on extremities both
at once. With so many contradictions I would hold, there
is, equally, an opportunity. A joy that is so splendid, and a
most cruel pain. Absolutism, of this or that stripe, so *sure*
of the escapes, is mistaken for a taste of the truth. And I
remain in the end a fumbling boy.

So, physically, with an openness of heart, we may hold
each other in sympathy with what will be. Without these
confidences life becomes an exhausting unhappiness. Gratitude alone can suffice for us to live. We push the stone together, calmly, while seeing when our time is up. We may
grow less afraid in each other's arms, putting aside the grim
things for a short while before they come. We two dead
things may live . . .

I tremble at what's here, so soon, so pointed: haunting
and corroding me. When I do, I will die wearing two faces.

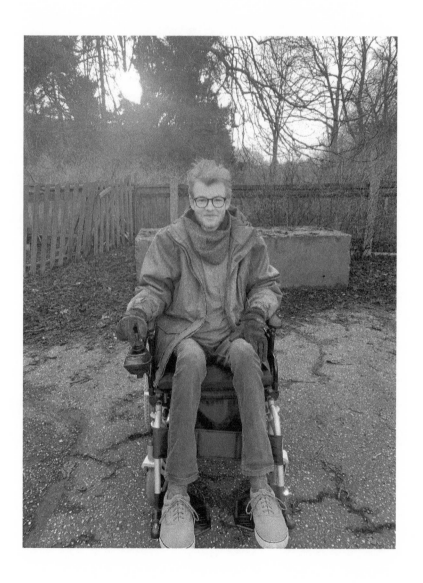

Jake Goldsmith is a writer with cystic fibrosis and the founder of The Barbellion Prize, a book prize for ill and disabled authors.

Lightning Source UK Ltd.
Milton Keynes UK
UKHW010918160522
403010UK00001B/36